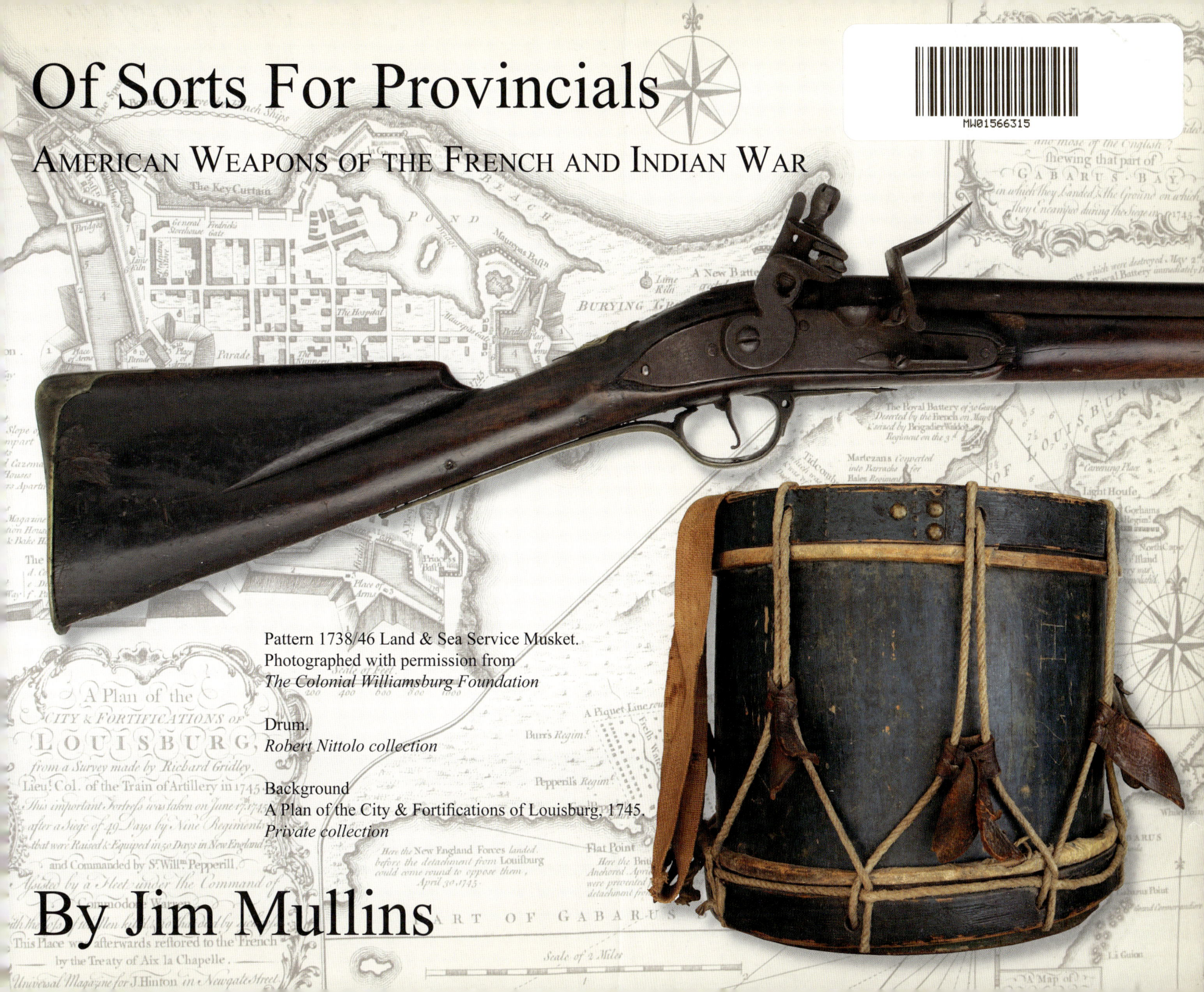

Of Sorts For Provincials

American Weapons of the French and Indian War

Pattern 1738/46 Land & Sea Service Musket.
Photographed with permission from
The Colonial Williamsburg Foundation

Drum.
Robert Nittolo collection

Background
A Plan of the City & Fortifications of Louisburg, 1745.
Private collection

By Jim Mullins

Published in the United States by:

Track of the Wolf, Inc.
18308 Joplin Street N.W.
Elk River, MN 55330-1773
www.trackofthewolf.com

Tel: 763-633-2500
Fax: 763-633-2550

Copyright © Track of the Wolf, Inc. 2008

All rights reserved. Except for use in review, no part of this book may be reproduced

or transmitted in any form or by any means, electronic or mechanical, including

photocopying and recording, or by an information storage or retrieval system

without written consent from the publisher.

All correspondence concerning this book should be addressed to Track of the Wolf, Inc.

ISBN			978-0-9765797-3-1

Editor:		Bryan Kennedy

Designer:		Ryan R. Gale

Front Cover:	*A Prospective Plan of the Battle fought near Lake George*
			on the 8th of September 1755.
			by Samuel Blodget
			Courtesy The Colonial Williamsburg Foundation

			Dutch musket, *Jim Mullins collection*

			George Washington in the Uniform of a British Colonial Colonel, c. 1772. by Charles Willson Peale
			Washington-Custis-Lee Collection, Washington and Lee University, Lexington, Virginia.

Unhappy provincials! If success attends where you are joined with the regulars, they claim all the honour, though not a tenth part your number: if disgrace, it is all yours, though you happen to be but a small part of the whole, and have no command; as if regulars were in their natures invincible when not mixed with provincials, and provincials of no kind of value without regulars...

Attributed to *"a New-Englandman"* as quoted in:
Some Observations on the Two Campaigns against the Cherokee Indians, in 1760 and 1761 CHARLES-TOWN: Printed and Sold by Peter Timothy MDCCLXIL

This book is dedicated to my maternal grandparents, Annie Christine and William Preston Webb, who inspired my love for history and the Virginia back country at an early age.

Acknowledgements

It is with sincere gratitude that my foremost thanks go to Erik Goldstein for his wealth of aid, advice and assistance provided during this project. I am also indebted to Ryan Gale, the principal photographer and graphic designer of this book, and my editor Bryan Kennedy, who also contributed greatly to the success of this project. In addition to Erik, Ryan, Bryan and the numerous institutions I visited during my research for this book, the following persons graciously provided valuable assistance:

Bill Ahern, Brandyn Charlton, Giles Cromwell, Mario Doreste, Chris Fox, Terry Gruber, Alan Gutchess, Wallace Gusler, Beth Hill, Matt Keagle, Jim Kochan, Carl Kuttruff, Steve Lalioff, Rebecca Morehouse, Barbara Mullins, Craig Nannos, Matt Nelson, George Neumann, Robert Nittolo, George Reilly, David Ripplinger, Steve Robertson, Joe Seymour, Scott Stephenson, Don Troiani, Richard Vernon, Jeff Wells.

Windham, William.
A plan of discipline, composed for the use of the militia of the county of Norfolk.
London, 1759
private collection

Contents

Foreword vi

Introduction vii

Royal Arms & Accouterments 1

Year by Year, 1754 – 1760:
    1754 11
    1755 17
    1756 19
    1758 23
    1759 29
    1760 35

Commercial and Civilian Arms and Accouterments:
    Non-Ordnance Cartridge Boxes 41
    Powder Horns and Shot Bags 43
    Fowling Pieces 49
    Light Arms 53
    Fusils 57
    Trade Fuzees 61
    Carbines 65
    Commercial Military Muskets 69
    American Composite Muskets 73
    Rifles 77
    Buccaneer Muskets 85
    Officer's Equipment 89

Colonies:
    Connecticut 97
    Georgia 103
    Maryland 105
    Massachusetts 117
    New Hampshire 123
    New Jersey 124
    New York 131
    North Carolina 133
    Pennsylvania 136
    Rhode Island 145
    South Carolina 149
    Virginia 161

Conclusion 180

Appendix 181

Glossary 182

Bibliography 183

Index 185

Foreword

It can be said that the Brown Bess musket is the sweetheart of those who collect and study the arms of the America's colonial wars. Her beauty, intrigue and raw appeal put Bess at the top of today's desirability list. But what of her sisters, cousins and friends? While paying appropriate homage to the standard Anglo-American soldier's firearm, Jim Mullins has done what no other arms scholar has yet attempted in such detail, and answered that question. Through *Of Sorts For Provincials*, he has heaped much-deserved attention on the commercial muskets, carbines, trade guns, parts guns, hunting guns, edged weapons and accouterments used by the colonial forces, both regular and irregular, during the French & Indian War. Within, we learn that Bess' relations and associates are just as historic, interesting and attractive as she is.

Rather than relying on supposition or imagination, Mullins has identified these diverse weapon types and their adjunct accessories strictly through the use of documentary and archaeological evidence in addition to that offered by the objects themselves. By no means are any of these avenues of study complete or exhaustive, but the data presented within this volume accurately reflects the manner in which these absolutely desperate American colonists were armed and equipped during the conflict.

More than just a clever title chosen from a period quote, the phrase *Of Sorts For Provincials* is an perfect expression for the smorgasbord of material, from the highest quality to the lowest imaginable, collected for the use of the Provincials. To us, the thought of units going into combat with third-hand worn out Dutch muskets, others dating to the late 17th century, and the refuse of numerous armories & stores on their persons, would seem almost comical if the situation wasn't such a frenetic crisis.

Somehow, the 21st century collector of arms has come to think of non-regulation arms & material, not issued by the Board of Ordnance out of the Tower of London or Dublin Castle, as second rate in both historical quality and desirability. Through Mullins' research, conducted in archives, libraries and museums on both sides of the Atlantic, we now know this modern ethic is flawed. Much like a well rounded, healthy diet includes all food groups, so must a collection or study of the material culture of the era. Within the covers of *Of Sorts For Provincials*, one will find a nicely balanced menu of what the primary source evidence has shown to be the, at-times unlikely, reality of the American armaments during French & Indian War. And what a tasty treat it is!

Erik Goldstein
Curator of Mechanical Arts & Numismatics
The Colonial Williamsburg Foundation
Williamsburg, Virginia
July 2008

Introduction

One of the most exotic and influential conflicts to change world history was the Seven Years War. Also known as the "French and Indian War" in North America, it raged from 1754 to 1763. Several varieties of professional and semi-professional soldiers, along with the militia, fought it. The most famous were the regulars of the British army, who generally enlisted for life or at least a substantial number of years. Provincials were soldiers raised by the individual colonies or "provinces." Serving under locally recruited officers with colonial commissions, provincial soldiers generally enlisted for a specific amount of time, normally a period of months or a campaign season. Their duties generally paralleled those of the Redcoats.

The Rangers differed from provincials in that they generally provided their own arms and were expected to scout in between fortified posts in order to scour the woods for the enemy. Least reliable of the fighting forces fielded by the British were the militia. The militia consisted of free white male citizens aged eighteen to sixty who were required by law to provide themselves with a gun, ammunition, and a sidearm, usually a sword, hatchet, or bayonet. Each colony's laws differed, but they frequently lacked force because of the relatively small fines for noncompliance. This, as well as the personal and financial implications of abandoning one's own family, crops, and property to serve frequently conspired to make the militia an inherently weak and unreliable force. Numerous county militias mustered unarmed, and sometimes refused to muster at all in times of crisis, heightening the need for Provincials and Rangers to provide assistance to the British regulars.

Although numerous works have been written on the Redcoats and the much vaunted Rangers, the participation of the provincials has gone largely overlooked. Almost every major event in the war was heavily impacted by provincials, and victory for the British in North America certainly would not have been possible without their contribution. Despite this, popular history frequently sweeps aside the impact of the provincial soldier whether good, bad, or indifferent in favor of the mythology and romance of the Redcoat and the Rangers. General John Forbes termed the officers of the Provincials *"an extream bad Collection of broken Innkeepers, Horse Jockeys, & Indian traders, and that the Men under them, are a direct copy of their Officers, nor can it well be otherwise, as they are a gathering from the scum of the worst of people in every Country, who have wrought themselves up, into a panick at the very name of Indians who at the same time are more infamous cowards, than any other race of mankind."*
(Writings of General John Forbes, page 205)

Little information on the specific types of arms provincial soldiers of British North America used has been published. This work is an attempt to compile and consolidate as much information as possible on that subject. Delving deeper into the subject produces far more questions than answers. Records are scanty, frequently vague and at times nearly inaccessible, not to mention the inherent challenges in simply reading the sometimes illegible handwriting. With this in mind, the original author's spelling and punctuation have been left intact. All quotations are italicized, and all square bracketed notations are those of the author. This book includes all known Royal shipments of small arms to North America from 1754 to 1763, numbering at least 1,000 stands, that were not intended primarily for British regulars. Dual shipments for provincials and regulars are included, and the nature of the shipment is noted when known. Smaller shipments and private or commercial purchases that can be identified are listed on an individual basis for each colonial government that received them.

Royal Arms and accoutrement shipments to North American Provincials in the French and Indian War

In mid-eighteenth century Britain and her colonies, official arms shipments originated from the Board of Ordnance, which was headquartered in the Tower of London. The Board of Ordnance oversaw arms procurement, production, storage, and dispersal for the land and sea forces of Great Britain. In the first decades of the eighteenth century, the colonel of a British regiment decided which firearms would be purchased by his agent for his regiment. At times cheap and inferior arms were procured, much to the detriment of the unit that received them. By the third decade of the eighteenth century, this practice had been abolished in favor of a standard "Pattern" or style of firearm for the British regulars. These pattern arms brought about standardization of ammunition, quality and to a limited extent, interchangeable parts. Some vestiges of the older procurement methods persisted for items such as cartridge pouches and hangers (short swords sometimes carried by infantrymen), these remained at the discretion of the regiment's colonel and purchasing agents.

Unless someone exerted great influence in the government, arms were generally issued to North America only in times of crisis. These shipments themselves tended to be infrequent, sporadic, and generally not the best sort that were available. Colonial governments traditionally received obsolete and older arms from Britain for provincial defense, as did British units serving in North America. Newer, high-quality arms were traditionally reserved for regiments closer to England. A memorandum sent to Governor and General William Shirley from the officers of the newly raised 50th and 51st Foot entitled *"The Memorial of the Field Officers of Major General Shirley, and Major General Sir William Pepperrell's Regiments of Foot."* noted *"That we think it our indispensible Duty to represent to your Excellency the Insufficiency of the Arms and Accoutrements of both Regiments. The Locks being wore out and the Hammers so soft, that notwithstanding repeated repairs they are almost unfit for Service, particularly Sir William Pepperrell's Regiment being old Dutch Arms. The holes of the Pouches and Boxes are so small that they cannot receive the Cartridge, nor is there Substance of the Wood, to widen them sufficiently, The Leather Scanty and bad likewise."*[1] North American Ordnance comptroller James Furnis noted in 1757 that *"many of those Arms issued by the Commissarys to the Provincial Forces differ from those received of the Kings Pattern, and are very indifferent Arms."*[2]

---

[1] *Public Records Office (PRO) CO, 5/46.* undated but included with other correspondence dated Sepr. 28th, 1755.

[2] *Furnis Letter book.* 9th February, 1757, page 70.

A Stand of Arms

Firearms were issued to infantry regiments, ships, and garrisons as complete sets, or "stands", meaning that all of the basic components and accouterments needed to operate the firearm were included. These components consisted of the firearm itself, a socket bayonet that fit the gun, a sling, a cartridge or "cartouch" box with a waist belt, a bayonet scabbard and a frog (a sliding leather strap that attached the bayonet scabbard to the waist belt that carried the box and bayonet scabbard).

Lead musket ball, c. 1754.
From a Braddock Road site.
Shown actual size.
Private collection

Paper cartridge.
Date unknown, likely 18th century.
Shown actual size.
Robert Nittolo collection

Pattern 1727 Land Service Bayonet and scabbard, c. 1727 – 1740.
Private collection

American Weapons of the French and Indian War

Above left
Cartouch box, bottom view,
c. 1750 – 1784.
Private collection

Above right
Cartouch box, belt, and frog,
c. 1760 – 1784.
Military & Historical Image Bank
www.historicalimagebank.com

An eighteen hole cartouch box, c. 1760 – 1784.
Giles and Carolyn Cromwell collection

Unlike the more expensive and substantial white buff leather slings and belts frequently purchased by the regular regiments, the accouterments from the Tower were scanty blackened "tanned" leather, and therefore less costly. The cartouch box was a simple wooden block drilled for nine, twelve, eighteen or twenty four holes, covered by a leather flap that was nailed to the rear of the box. Two thin leather strips nailed to the front of the box served as loops for the waistbelt, which carried the frog and bayonet scabbard.

American Weapons of the French and Indian War

A nine hole cartouch box recovered from the *HMS Invincible*, which sank in 1758. *Robert Nittolo collection*

Pattern 1730 musket, c. 1730 – 1740.
Overall length: 63 ½", barrel length: 46", caliber: .78.
Robert Nittolo collection

Pattern 1730 Muskets

The original "King's Pattern" musket featured decorative stock carving, a single bridled lock, Dutch style brass trigger guard, wooden rammer and originally lacked a nose band.[3] Although not commonly called "Brown Bess" in the period, this pattern was the stylistic origin point for British military muskets well into the nineteenth century and was the main arm used by British Regulars in North America in the decades prior to the French and Indian War. A specimen of this type that had been imported in 1754[4] and subsequently captured from the 50th Regiment was recovered from the wreckage of the French ship *Le Machault* which sunk in 1760; having served both sides of the conflict.[5]

---

[3] *Pattern Dates for British Ordnance, 1718 – 1783*, pages 55-56.

[4] *Military Affairs in North America*, page 486.

[5] *The Socket Bayonet in the British Army, 1687 – 1783*, page 62.

American Weapons of the French and Indian War

The lock is engraved "Farmer, 1729".

Pattern 1730 muskets featured a single bridled lock.

Of Sorts For Provincials

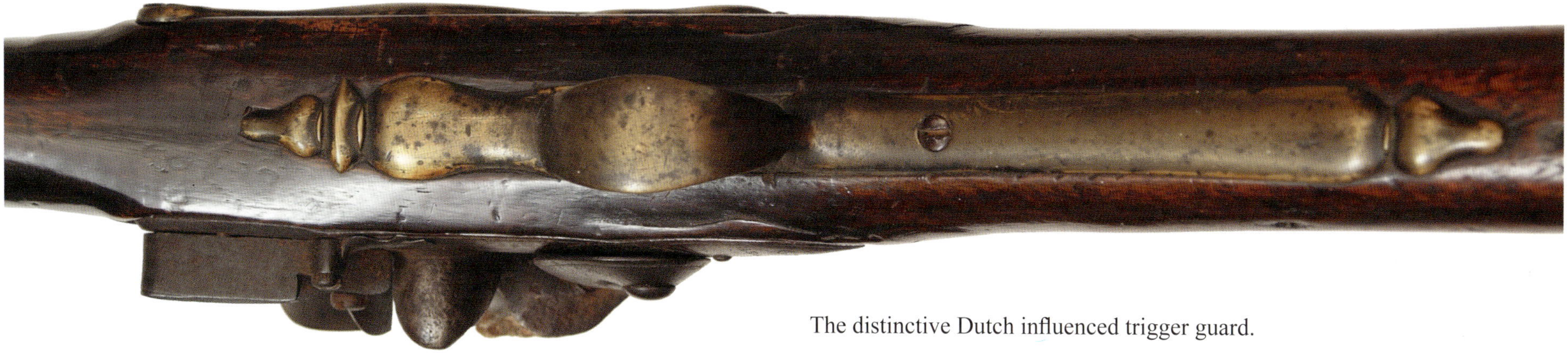

American Weapons of the French and Indian War

The distinctive Dutch influenced trigger guard.

Originally configured for a larger diameter wooden rammer, this musket has been altered during it's working life to utilize a metal rammer.

Pattern 1727 bayonet.
Private collection

Variations of bayonet markings:

American Weapons of the French and Indian War

Brass-mounted Dutch musket, c. 1730 – 1740.
Overall length: 61 3/8", barrel length: 45 7/8", caliber: .78.
Jim Mullins collection

1754

Escalating tensions over who controlled the Ohio Country prompted both the English and French to send forces to fortify the area. Despite an initial victory over a small French party, the English army (composed of inexperienced and ill-equipped Virginians under the command of a young George Washington) were defeated at Fort Necessity, and retreated from the Ohio Country. The French army further strengthened their position by building Fort Duquesne at the site of modern day Pittsburgh, Pennsylvania and the stage was set for a world wide conflict. While these events were unfolding, requests for munitions and assistance began to arrive from the colonies of Virginia and North Carolina in England. On *"Sat: Night June 29th 1754"* a warrant was issued for *"3000 Musquets and Bayonets of Dutch Fabrick, 3000 Tanned Leather Slings for the same, 3000 Cartouch Boxes with Belts and Frogs, 3000 Sea Service Swords with Tanned Leather belts together with 120 Halberts and 80 Drums."*[6] Two thousand stands were distributed to Virginia and North Carolina received the balance. In addition, two infantry regiments (the 44th and 48th Foot) under the newly appointed Commander-in-chief of North America, Major General Edward Braddock, as well as a sizable train of artillery and arms for two more infantry regiments to be raised in the colonies (the 50th and 51st) were put aboard ships for North America.

---

[6] *War Office (W.O.)*, 55/354, page 305.

American Weapons of the French and Indian War

Dutch muskets from the 1741 purchase featured single bridled locks and faceted pans (see page 15).

Fragment of a Dutch musket butt plate, c. 1740, recovered from the site of Fort Ticonderoga.
Collection of the Fort Ticonderoga Museum

Dutch bayonet, c. 1730 – 1740.
Private collection

Fragments of a Dutch musket trigger guard in the archeological collection of Fort Ticonderoga.
Collection of the Fort Ticonderoga Museum

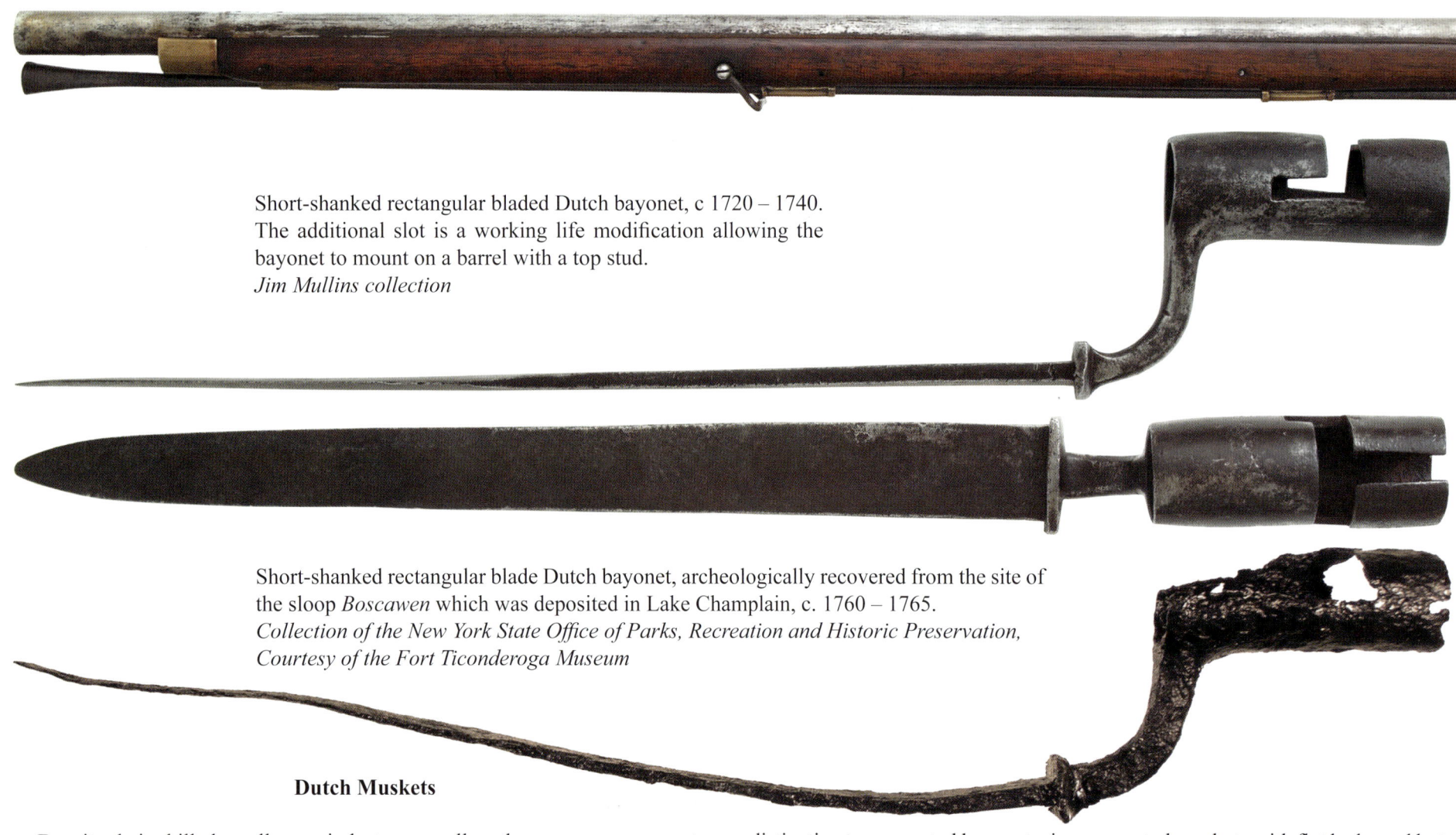

Short-shanked rectangular bladed Dutch bayonet, c 1720 – 1740. The additional slot is a working life modification allowing the bayonet to mount on a barrel with a top stud.
Jim Mullins collection

Short-shanked rectangular blade Dutch bayonet, archeologically recovered from the site of the sloop *Boscawen* which was deposited in Lake Champlain, c. 1760 – 1765.
Collection of the New York State Office of Parks, Recreation and Historic Preservation, Courtesy of the Fort Ticonderoga Museum

Dutch Muskets

Despite their skilled small arms industry as well as the necessary raw materials, the British gun trade could not always keep up with demand. In order to remedy wartime shortages, arms were purchased from the "Dutch", a loose term that covered the modern nations of the Netherlands, Germany, Belgium, Austria and Switzerland. Large quantities of various Dutch arms and gun barrels were purchased in 1706, 1715, 1741 and 1745.[7] Three main types appear to have been purchased, the earliest being iron-mounted muskets with round locks and distinctive top-mounted bayonets, iron-mounted muskets with flat locks and bottom-mounted bayonets, and later, brass-mounted muskets with bottom-mounted bayonets. Most of the Dutch arms that can be positively placed in America during the colonial period lack identifiable maker's marks, but the cities of Liege and Maastricht are represented. Dutch parts are found at numerous archeological sites, with many variations in furniture and bayonet styles.

---
[7] *The Socket Bayonet in the British Army*, by Erik Goldstein, pages 84 – 85.

American Weapons of the French and Indian War

Left
Dutch side plate, c. 1720 – 1740.
Recovered from the site of Fort Ticonderoga.
Collection of the Fort Ticonderoga Museum

Pattern 1730 / 1740 Long Land musket, c. 1740 – 1742.
Overall length: 61 $^{11}/_{16}$", barrel length: 45 $^{1}/_{2}$", caliber: .77.
Photographed with permission from
The Colonial Williamsburg Foundation

1755

Following the 1754 defeat of English forces in the Ohio Country, plans were made to eject the French from North America. Major General Braddock and his army arrived in Hampton, Virginia and began landing a sizable train of artillery and supplies. Bolstered by provincials from North Carolina, Virginia, and Maryland, Braddock's army pushed towards Fort Duquesne. Another force composed of the 50th and 51st regiments along with provincials attacked the French on Lake Ontario. An additional army fought the French at Crown Point and a fourth army, composed of New England provincials and a small contingent of regulars, attacked the French in Nova Scotia. In order to supply the New England men for their expedition to Nova Scotia, 2,000 *"Land Muskets of the King's Pattern wth double Bridle Locks & Wood Rammers…Bayonets with Scabbards…Musquet Slings of Tann'd Leather…Cartouch Boxes with Straps…12 Holes…"*[8] were consigned to William Shirley Esq., Governor of His Majesty's Province of Massachusetts Bay in America. Later references to these arms indicate they featured *"Old Pattern Nosebands."*[9] In September of 1755, Shirley noted that these arms were *"consign'd to me the last Spring."*[10]

---

[8] October 13th, 1755. *W.O. 55/411*, page 77.

[9] *W.O. 47/46*, page 143.

[10] Shirley to Robinson. September 28th, 1755. *PRO CO, 5/46. Correspondence of Shirley*, page 298.

American Weapons of the French and Indian War

Ordnance view and proof marks.

Pattern 1730 / 1740 muskets often featured double bridled locks.

1756

A formal declaration of war against France was issued one year later, and John Campbell, Earl of Loudon, replaced the unfortunate Braddock as Commander-in-Chief in North America, with General James Abercromby appointed second in command. In the wake of the disastrous defeat of the Braddock expedition in 1755, a dramatic change in arms dispersal procedures followed. For the coming campaign, an arms depot in North America was established in lieu of the normal system of issuing arms directly from the Tower in London. A series of royal warrants were written for issuing 10,000 stands of arms and ammunition for Service in North America & establishing a small staff to tend to the shipment. They would consist of *"1 Comptroller, 1 Storekeeper and Paymaster, 1 Clerk of Stores, and 2 Armourers."*[11] The Comptroller was Mr. James Furnis, Francis Stephens served in the capacity of Storekeeper and Paymaster and the depot was set up in Boston, Massachusetts.

In the spring of 1756, William Shirley, then serving as both Governor of Massachusetts and overall commander of British colonial military efforts in North America, received word that the *"10,000 stands of Arms, & proportion of Ammunition sent by his Majesty to Boston for the use of the Colonies, according to the Discretion of the Commander in Chief of his Forces in North America, are now arriv'd, & are under the Care of the Comptroller of Ordnance settled by the Board at that place."*[12] This shipment consisted entirely of *"Land Service Muskets of the King's Pattern with Brass Furniture, Double Bridle Locks Wood Rammers with Bayonets &Scabbards and Tann'd Leather Slings…Cartouch Boxes with Straps of 12 Holes…"*[13]

---

[11] *W.O.* 55/12, page 2-4.

[12] Shirley to Sharpe, April 24th, 1756. *Correspondence of Sharpe.*

[13] *W.O.* 55/412, page 3. Nov. 12th, 1755.

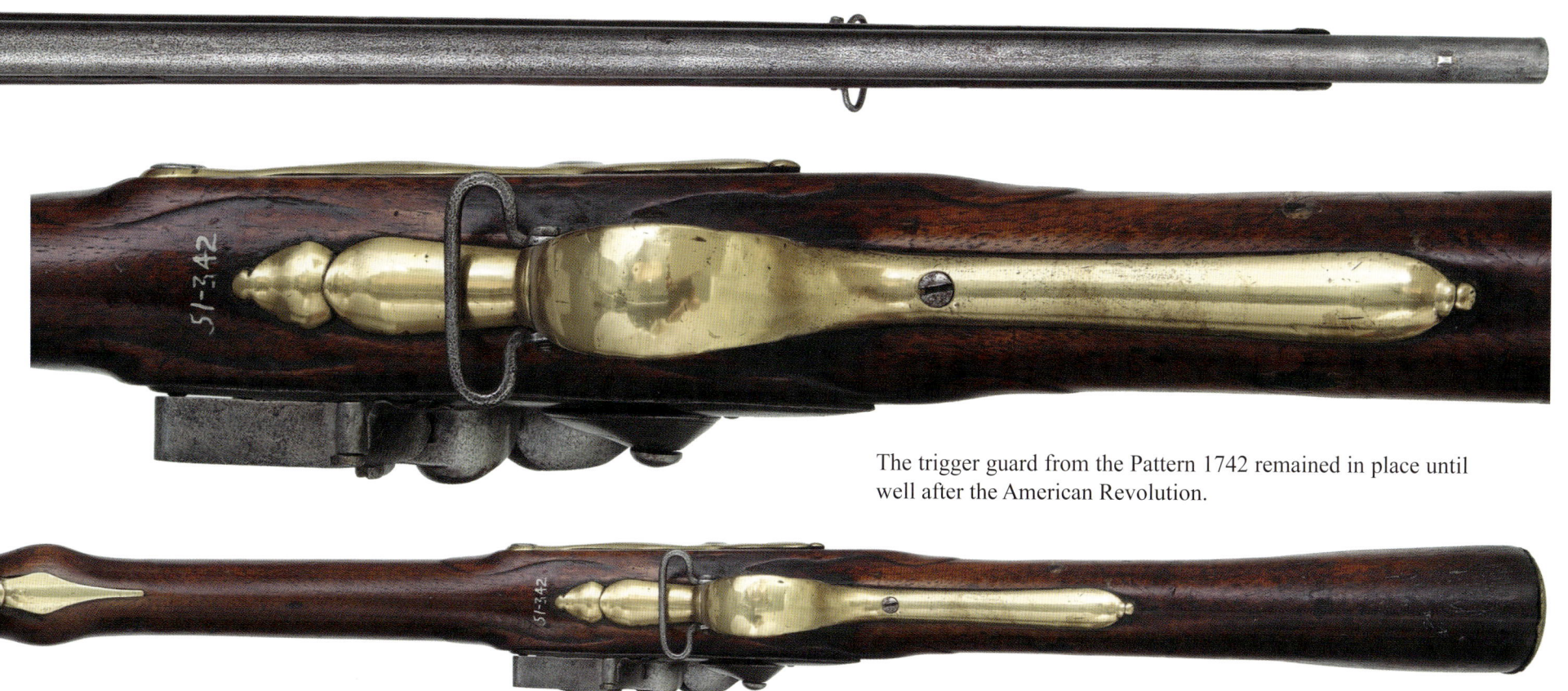

The trigger guard from the Pattern 1742 remained in place until well after the American Revolution.

Shirley sought to distribute to the colonies, except Virginia and Connecticut, *"Arms for four sevenths of the Men, they now raise: I am oblig'd to furnish his Majesty's four Regiments of Regulars immediately with 1200 Stands; and the 10,000 stands will hold out for no larger a proportion, leaving only 800 stands in the Stores for Extraordinary Contingencies."*

The individual colonies were *"to return the Arms at the End of the present Service, for wch they are lent to the Province, into his Majesty's Stores at Boston, pursuant to the Directions of the Board of Ordnance there to be kept by their Officers, as a Magazine for the use of the Colonies, which shall want them."*[14] By September 28, 1756, Shirley came to the conclusion that *"The sending of what Arms and Cloathing shall be judg'd proper to North America, if sent to New York instead of Boston, would save a fortnight or three Weeks time, as the Men may receive them at Albany, where the Governor of New York may, upon their Arrival there, be directed to send them."* Shirley recommended that *"as a Measure absolutely necessary, and of the utmost Consequence to his Majesty's Service, the establishing of a public Magazine of Small Arms and Ammunition in each Province; And I think, Sir, that 50,000 Stands of Arms at least, should be sent over for that purpose; as I believe that Number is scarce the fourth part of the Fighting Men, in his Majesty's several Colonies in North America...Besides this, Sir, I would recommend the Establishment of a public Magazine of Artillery, Arms, Ammuniton etc., for the use of his Majesty's Regular Troops; to be fix'd at New York, and to be in proportion to the number of Corps etc. his Majesty shall think proper to keep up in North America."*[15]

Ironically, a contemporary Ordnance report on the *"State of Small Arms in Great Britain for Land Service"* listed *"52,707 muskets"* as of September 6, 1755, throwing some doubt on the possibility of compliance with the request even if the

---

[14] Shirley to Sharpe, April 24th, 1756. *Correspondence of Sharpe.*

[15] *Shirley to Henry Fox,* Boston, April 12th, 1756.

Ordnance bayonet, c. 1740 – 1750.
Private collection

Pattern 1742 Muskets

Truly the workhorse of the French and Indian War, Pattern 1742 muskets represent almost half of all arms imported into America from Tower stores. More sturdy and in some respects a simplified version of the earlier King's pattern arms of 1730, this firelock featured a double-bridled lock, a different trigger guard and was frequently fitted with a brass nose band to slow wear on the fore end of the stock.[19]

Ordnance had been so inclined.[16] Once the 10,000-stand shipment was delivered, numerous complaints were received about the condition of these arms. Virginia's Lieutenant Governor Robert Dinwiddie noted that the arms received in Virginia arrived *"in a very rusty Condition, and it w'd appear they had been under Water for Months."*[17] Comptroller Furnis wrote to his superiors in the Board of Ordnance that this supply did not last long. On 16, July 1756, Furnis explained that there now remained *"out of the 10,000 Stand of Arms under the Charge of Mr. Turner 1549 together with Bayonets Cartouch boxes & ct. as also 1166 more from General Winslows and Lt Colonel Scott's Provincials, most of which are in a very bad Condition…"*[18]

---

[16] *Pargellis*, page 474.

[17] October 28th, 1756. Dinwiddie to Lord Loudon. *Dinwiddie Papers*, page 532.

[18] *W.O. 47/48*, page 272.

[19] *Pattern Dates for British Ordnance, 1718 – 1783*, page 56.

American Weapons of the French and Indian War

22

Pattern 1738 / 1746 Land & Sea Service Musket, c. 1746.
Overall length: 61", barrel length: 45 $^{15}/_{16}$", caliber: .78.
Photographed with permission from
The Colonial Williamsburg Foundation

The American escutcheon marked "1759" is a decorative working life addition.

1758

The campaigns of 1758 featured another expedition against Fort Duquesne, under the command of General John Forbes, and a failed attack on Ticonderoga, led by the new British commander General Abercromby. A successful attack on Louisburg was mounted under the command of Jeffery Amherst, and additionally the French Fort Frontenac surrendered to John Bradstreet, which in turn hastened the demise of Fort Duquesne. In order to facilitate these campaigns, a warrant was signed by William Pitt on January 5th, 1758, stipulating *"For New York 12,000 …Musquets with Wood Rammers - Bayonets and Tann'd Leather slings."*[20]

These firearms were further broken down into the following categories in another document:

Long Land Service with Wooden Rammers – 2,798
Dutch with do. – 6,207
With Flat locks do. – 1,866
of Various Patterns – 1,237
Total – 12,108 [21]

A portion of these arms were then directed to be sent *"For Pensilvania 2,000… Musquets with Wood Rammers- Bayonets and Tann'd Leather slings."*[22]

---

[20] *W.O.* 55/412, page 191.
[21] *W.O.* 47/50, page 427. December 23rd, 1757.
[22] Warrant signed by William Pitt dated January 5th, 1758. *W.O.* 55/412, page 191.

The lock is marked "I VAUGHAN 1745"

Arms procurement and dispersal proved to be a complete fiasco in 1758 due to a misunderstanding as to whether the colonies or the Crown were providing arms, and to the extreme tardiness of the arms sent from England. The store ships did not arrive until June of that year, severely hampering the progress of both General Abercromby in New York and General Forbes in Pennsylvania. Despite a royal proclamation announcing that the colonies need only raise, clothe, and pay for their quotas of men for the ensuing campaign, only 12,000 additional stands of arms were shipped to North America, far less than would be necessary to equip all the men involved. This was likely due to a fundamental misunderstanding of the actual supply at hand in North America and the priority of arms necessary for campaigns in Europe. Although thousands of arms had been arriving in the years prior, many were lost to theft, desertion, capture, and poor maintenance. These circumstances forced British officials and some of the colonies themselves to purchase large quantities of arms in America for the provincials, driving up demand and creating a handsome profit for the merchants who had imported them.

"1746" and Broad Arrow markings on the interior of a Land & Sea Service butt plate in the archeological collection of Fort Ticonderoga.
Collection of the Fort Ticonderoga Museum

Ordnance Comptroller James Furnis reported to his superiors that *"Since I wrote to our Honours on 27th April last 2246 Musquets & ca. have been purchased at this place [New York], and sent to Albany for Service of the Provincial Troops assembling there, which with those before at Albany, and Fort Edward will amount to 6500."*[23] General Forbes found himself in a similar predicament and wrote that *"As the Store Ship was so late of Coming in, I was obliged to purchase a great many Arms, Tents & c, for the Provinicalls."*[24]

Most of the arms types included in the 1758 shipment can be identified through archeology and Tower inventories. The varieties included seem to indicate that this shipment was an opportunity for the Tower to unload cast-off, obsolete, and odd sorts of arms in North America, likely in order to make room for the large scale production of new pattern arms that was in full swing in England.

Muskets of the King's Pattern or *"Long Land Service with Wooden Rammers"* comprised the first category. Given the vague description, this could include pattern 1730 muskets in addition to later types. Over 6,000 Dutch muskets with wooden rammers were also included in this shipment. A document entitled the *"State of Small Arms…in Store at the Tower"* dated 31 December, 1754, notes that all of the Dutch muskets in storage featured *"brass furniture"*[25] making it likely that all of the Dutch arms that were included featured brass furniture. Some variations seem to have been represented, as multiple styles of brass "Dutch" mounts (trigger guards, side plates, and butt plates) have been uncovered at Ticonderoga and Crown Point.

---

[23] *Furnis Letter book*, 1st June, 1758, page 137.
[24] Forbes to Pitt. *Writings of General John Forbes*, page 118.
[25] *W.O.* 47/45, page 23 – 24.

The portion of the arms with *"Flat locks"* probably included obsolete "Marine" pattern muskets (which Bailey terms the "Pattern 1738 and 1746 Long Land and Sea Service Musket" in his *British Military Small Arms*) as the distinctive, three-screw side plates and other furniture from this pattern have been recovered from Fort Ticonderoga. As for the small number of remaining arms *"of Various patterns"*, little is known other than that they were comprised of obsolete *"Musquets with Wood Rammers - Bayonets and Tann'd Leather slings."*[26]

Distinctive Land & Sea Service musket trigger guard fragments from the sloop *Boscawen* which sank in Lake Champlain c. 1760 – 1765. Collection of the New York State Office of Parks, Recreation and Historic Preservation, Courtesy of the Fort Ticonderoga Museum.

---

[26] Pitt's Warrant dated January 5th, 1758. W.O. 55/412, page 191.

Above
Land & Sea musket side plate recovered from the site of Fort Ticonderoga, marked "33". The oval indentation was a thumb rest used to aid in gripping the musket at the one handed position of "Poise" from the manual exercise.
Courtesy of the Fort Ticonderoga Museum.

Right
The position of "Poise Your Firelock" from the manual exercise as illustrated in Benjamin Cole's *The Soldier's Pocket-Companion, or the Manual Exercise of our British Foot* (London, 1746).
Private collection

1738 and 1746 Long Land and Sea Service Muskets

A strange and ungainly hybrid combining characteristics of contemporary land and sea service muskets, the outdated marine musket was inventoried as suitable *"for Land or Sea Service"* in a document entitled *"State of Small Arms... in Store at the Tower."*[27] It was imported for use in the 1758 campaign. The musket's distinctive brass hardware has been found near Fort Ticonderoga.[28] This particular gun exhibits decorative additions from an unknown eighteenth century American user.

---

[27] December 31st, 1754. *W.O. 47/45*, page 23 – 24.
[28] *Pattern Dates for British Ordnance, 1718 – 1783*, page 58.

American Weapons of the French and Indian War

Land & Sea musket side plate marked "26".
Note the similarity of the markings to the example recovered from the *Boscawen* shown on page 27.

Carbine by Thomas Hatcher of London, c. 1745 – 1750.
Possibly an example of carbines "by the trade" procured by the Ordnance.
Overall length: 52 3/8", barrel length: 36 5/8", caliber: .70.
Photographed with permission from
The Colonial Williamsburg Foundation

1759

At the end of 1758, Sir Jeffrey Amherst was promoted to overall commander of British forces in North America. Plans for the 1759 campaign called for attacks on Montreal and Quebec as well as an expedition to retake Oswego and to take Fort Niagara. Ticonderoga, Crown Point, and Quebec all fell to British forces and the French largely withdrew to Montreal.

In December of 1758, 4,000 muskets and 4,000 carbines arrived in New York. On May 5, 1759, 1,228 of these carbines were ordered issued to the Light Infantry companies within the Regular Regiments in North America, as well as the 80th regiment, also known as Gage's Light Armed Foot.[29] These arms were cavalry carbines issued *"without bayonets"*, although this situation was quickly changed *"...The Light infantry of the army are to have their bayonets, as the want of ammunition may sometimes be supplied with that weapon; and, because no man should leave his post, under pretence that all his cartridges are fired, in most attacks by night, it must be remembered, that bayonets are preferable to fire."*[30]

---

[29] Amherst to Furnis, May 5th, 1759. *W.O.* 34/70, page 44.
[30] *Captain John Knox's Journal.* July 5th, 1759. Volume 1, Page 400.

Ordnance proof marks on the barrel.

Ordnance Carbines

The Light infantry companies had previously been fielding with lightened British and captured French muskets and returned their old arms to Ordnance stores.[31] This rearming was an attempt to put the Light Infantry companies on a similar footing to their lightly armed and accoutered French and Indian foes. It is highly unlikely that provincials received any carbines from this shipment, although Amherst sent 200 for the use of Indians to Sir William Johnson.[32] The carbines, although much handier, seemed to have proved unpopular with some units and were likely not sturdy enough for active service. After less than a year, some carbines were being traded in for full sized muskets. *"The light infantry companies…are ordered to be completed with firelocks instead of short carbines, at their own request."*[33]

Five distinct patterns of carbines (both with and without bayonets) were in kept in Tower stores prior to the French and Indian War for use by mounted troops and the Royal Artillery.[34] Although variations existed, and some (such as this specimen) were *"made by the trade."*[35] These carbines featured a 37 inch barrel and were "carbine" bore of approximately .65 caliber.

[31] Amherst to Furnis. May 5th, 1759. *W.O.* 34/70, page 44.

[32] Amherst to Johnson. May 23rd, 1759. *The papers of Sir William Johnson*, volume 13, page 44.

[33] *Captain John Knox's Journal*. February 7th, 1760. Volume 2, page 337.

[34] *State of Small Arms…in the Tower…*January 14th, 1755. *W.O.* 47/45, page 24.

[35] *Ibid.*

American Weapons of the French and Indian War

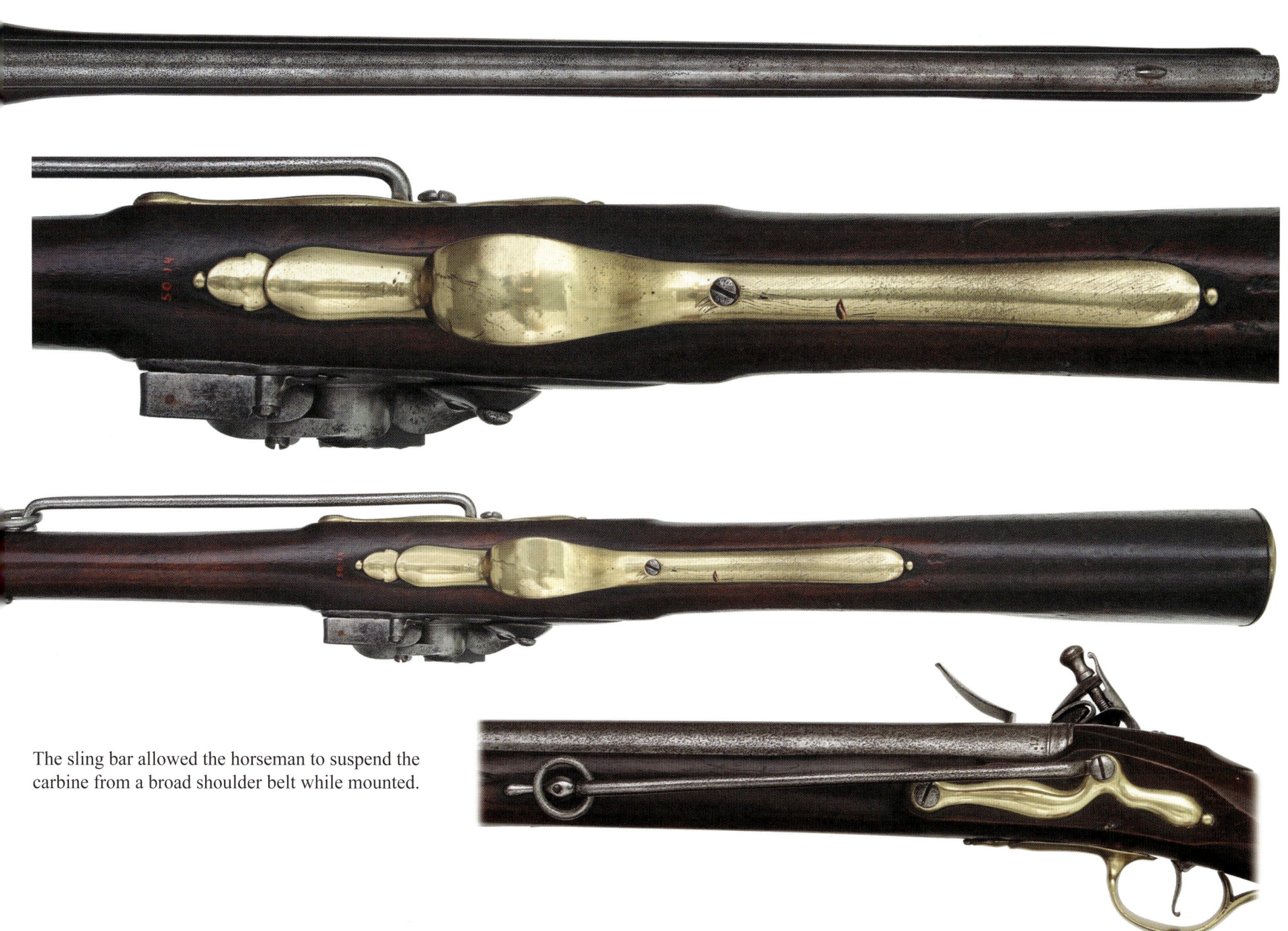

The sling bar allowed the horseman to suspend the carbine from a broad shoulder belt while mounted.

Ordnance carbine bayonet and scabbard, c. 1755 – 1760.
Private collection

American Weapons of the French and Indian War

Marine or Militia musket, c. 1757 – 1760.
Overall length: 58 ½", barrel length: 42".
Giles and Carolyn Cromwell collection

1760

Three columns of British forces converged on Montreal while another army fought the once allied Cherokee tribe in the southern back country. Shipments of arms decreased dramatically and on January 8, 1760 *"2,000 Militia Muskets with Wood Rammers Bayonets and Scabbards…Cartouch Boxes Compleat…in 80 chests"*[36] were *"Laden on board the Free Mason…to be transported to New York…and there deliver'd to Mr. Francis Stephens Ordnance Storekeeper being for his Majestys service in North America."* Shipped on March 1st, they arrived in New York by July 1, 1760, and seem to have been the last major shipment of small arms for provincial use in North America during the war.

Marine or Militia muskets lacked wrist plates.

---

[36] *W.O.* 34/70, page 18.

American Weapons of the French and Indian War

Marine or Militia muskets featured 42 inch barrels, and initially lacked nose bands.

This abbreviated Marine or Militia musket's butt plate was anchored with a top screw.

A return dated April 3, 1762 compiled by Francis Stephens, the Ordnance Storekeeper and Paymaster in New York[37] lists the following (the first number denotes items that are serviceable, the second items that are repairable):

    Muskets-
    Kings Pattern- 5180 Serv.ble " 699 Rep.ble
    of Sorts for Provincials- 4465 " 1774
    French- " " 170

    Carbines of the Kings Pattern- 69 " 570
    Pistols wth Ribs…pairs- 43 " -

    Bayonets- Kings Pattern- 5063 " 2570
        Of Sorts- 1917 " -
        Carbine- 69 " 948

    Scabbards for- Musket- 7041 " -
        Carbine- 640 " -

    Cartouch Boxes-
    Musket
        24 Holes-13 " 65-
        18Do-3788 " 295 -
        12Do-4 " -
        9Do-10 " -
    Carbine of 18 Holes 983 " 242
    Straps for Do- 4898 " -
    Frogs for Do.- 4872 " -

[37] W.O. 34/70, page 32.

Marine or Militia Muskets

This last wartime return illustrates that the motley collection of non-regulation, outdated, and low-quality arms *"Of Sorts"* were provided for Provincials while the Regulation 'King's Pattern' arms were reserved for regulars, when supplies permitted. This return also shows that a large quantity of carbines with bayonets were also in British warehouses in North America, as well as some captured French arms.

The only type of current production firearm to be imported to America from the Tower during the French and Indian war, *"Short Musquets of the new Pattern for Marines or Militia"* featured a distinctive butt plate, a 42-inch barrel, and omitted the brass thumb piece and rammer tailpipe as cost saving measures. Two thousand stands with wooden rammers were shipped to New York in 1760.

The entry pipe was omitted as a cost savings measure on the Marine or Militia musket.

Ordnance bayonet, c. 1755 – 1760.
Private collection

Brass tip from a wooden ramrod.
Shown actual size.
Private collection

American Weapons of the French and Indian War

A flat side plate was a standard feature on the utilitarian Marine or Militia musket.

Commercial cartridge box, c. 1750 – 1830.
Robert Nittolo collection

Commercial and Civilian Arms and Accouterments of North American Provincials

Some provincial governments through foresight and necessity provided themselves with commercially-purchased arms and ammunition at the public expense, but the additional financial burden was sometimes unpopular even during wartime. A wide variety of arms and accouterments were generally available in the major cities during the period. Newspaper advertisements from Charleston, South Carolina, Philadelphia, New York, and Boston abound with imported arms and equipment. Supply could not always keep up with demand, most notably in Philadelphia after the defeat of Braddock, and virtually everywhere during the 1758 campaign. This in turn drove up prices considerably. Military style, commercially-manufactured muskets (frequently the products of the London-based firm of Richard Wilson), complete with bayonets, slings and cartouch boxes were imported alongside civilian fowling pieces, short carbines, slim fusees and captured foreign arms taken by privateers.

In addition to purchasing arms on the open market, some colonies impressed arms in order to equip their provincials when necessary.[38] Domestic arms production was limited during this period. Most American gunsmiths were simply repairing European arms or assembling parts that originated in Europe.

In addition to the firearms purchased by colonies on the commercial market for their provincial forces, wartime shortages caused several colonies to encourage recruits to bring their own personal arms and equipment, often for a bonus and guarantee that the gun would be paid for if damaged, lost, or destroyed. This policy was most prevalent in the colonies of New England where it appeared from the earliest stages of the war.

Non-Ordnance Cartridge Boxes

In addition to cartridge boxes from Ordnance stores, cartridge boxes were also imported and made domestically in America. Sold from shops like the "Sign of the Knapsack" in Philadelphia (as well as by more generalized merchants), these boxes at times featured tin tubes instead of wooden blocks.

---

[38] For examples see the *Virginia Journal of the House of Burgesses,* 1752 – 58 page 463 and *Journals of the House of Representatives of Massachusetts*, Volume XXXIII part 2 page 314 – 315.

Thirteen tin tubes fill the leather pouch. The flap is secured by a leather button. The belt is secured by a roller buckle. Although rare in 18th century Ordnance equipment and more common in the next century, roller buckles were utilized in some civilian leather goods.

An illustration showing the stamp which covers the body and flap of this pouch.

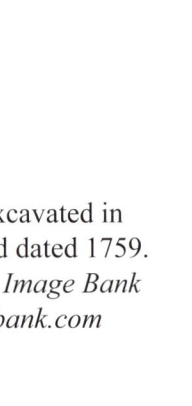

Left
Shot pouch, date unknown.
Wallace Gusler collection

Right
Knife and scabbard excavated in Philadelphia, scabbard dated 1759.
Military & Historical Image Bank
www.historicalimagebank.com

Powder Horns and Shot Bags

A frequent lack of suitable cartridge boxes, cartridge paper, variations in bore size and the nature of fighting in America led to the widespread usage of shot bags, or pouches, with powder horns by many Provincial soldiers. In June of 1758, Colonel Henry Bouquet wrote to General Forbes *"I have noticed a great inconvenience in the use of cartridges for them (provincials). They do not know how to make cartridges or rather they take too much time. In the woods they seldom have time or places suitable to make them. These cartridge boxes hold only 9 charges, some 12 which is not sufficient. I think that their powder horns and pouches for carrying bullets would be much more useful, keeping the*

Shot pouch, c. 1750 – 1850.
Photographed with permission from
The Colonial Williamsburg Foundation

cartridge box however, to use in case of a sudden or night attack."[39] "Shot bags" or "shot pouches" were small leather or linen canvas bags used to carry bullets and smaller shot. Captain John Knox described them as *"a leathern, or seal's skin bag, buckled round their waist, which hangs down before, contains bullets, and a smaller shot, of the size of full-grown peas: six or seven of which; with a ball, they generally load."*[40]

---

[39] Blackmore, *British Military Firearms*, page 68.

[40] *Captain John Knox's Journal*, July 12 – 13, 1757, page 34.

Meshach Taylor's horn, 1747.
Overall length: 12".
Photographed with permission from
The Colonial Williamsburg Foundation

The suckling fawn motif was common on eighteenth century powder horns.

Powder horns, and, to a lesser degree, powder flasks were utilized with the shot bag or pouch to carry gunpowder. At times the products of professional horn makers, these horns featuring turned wooden plugs, occasionally fitted with small mirrors, neatly crafted brass spouts or even *"a small compass fixed in the bottoms…by which to direct them, when they happen to lose themselves in the woods."*[41] Professionally-made utilitarian horns were purchased and issued in bulk, while other horns were made and decorated by their owners or other soldiers such as the famous John Bush. Designs, features, markings, and horn forms vary widely. The mixture of military and civilian arms with powder horns and cartouch boxes in the ranks could cause logistical problems when standard musket-sized cartridge ammunition was issued.

---

[41] *Captain John Knox's Journal*, July 12 – 13, 1757, page 34.

American Weapons of the French and Indian War

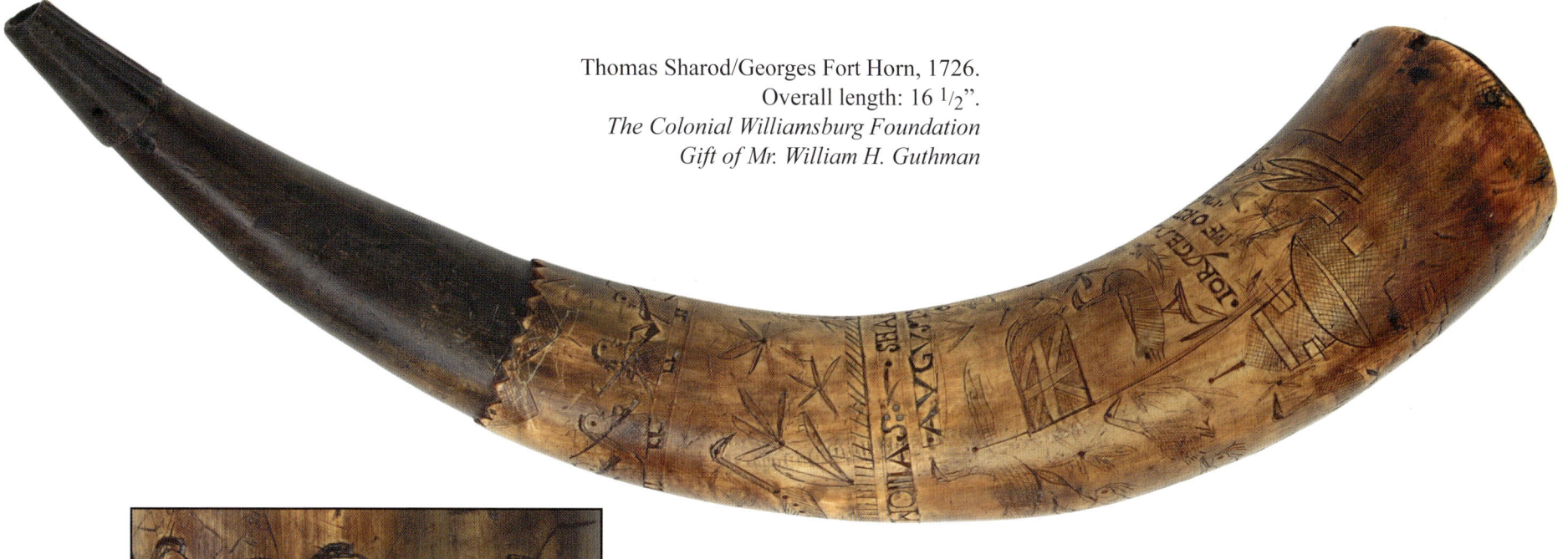

Thomas Sharod/Georges Fort Horn, 1726.
Overall length: 16 1/2".
The Colonial Williamsburg Foundation
Gift of Mr. William H. Guthman

Armed figures and other images adorn this horn.

Tin powder measure, c. 1750 – 1850.
The Colonial Williamsburg Foundation
Gift of Mr. Madison Grant

An entry from the Orderly Book of Massachusetts Lieutenant William Henshaw states that *"the Capt. or Commanding Officers of Companies see that the Balls fit the Mens Guns so that they run down the Barrels & to have Every thing Ready to March to Morrow morning by 5 Clock. Those that have not got Cartridges boxes must break their Cartridges & put there powder into there horns."*[42] In order to assure that a consistent safe charge of powder was taken from the horns, a measure or charger was frequently used with them. A document entitled *"A List of Goods purchased by Capt. Bosomworth and William West for the Cherokee Indians by Order of General Forbes"* indicates that the 500 powder horns purchased in Philadelphia in May of 1758 were each supplied with a *"Tin Measure."*[43]

---

[42] William Henshaw Orderly Book entry dated 31st of May, 1759, from *Transactions and Collections of the American Antiquarian Society: Manuscript Records of the French and Indian war in the Library of the Society*, Volume XI.

[43] *General John Forbes Headquarters Papers*, Alderman Library Manuscript Collection, University of Virginia.

Jacob Thomson's horn, 1760.
Overall length: 12".
Photographed with permission from
The Colonial Williamsburg Foundation

Tow and brick dust were used to clean and polish musket barrels.

Keeping the Firelock Clean

One of the most important duties of eighteenth century soldiers and "Armourers" was keeping their arms clean and functioning properly. An eighteenth century sporting treatise[44] goes into depth on the process of cleaning a musket. The treatise recommends that *"it is necessary the inside of the barrel, the touchhole and lock, be kept clean; and the springs and moving parts of the lock properly oiled. The barrel should be washed at least after every eighteen or twenty fires, where the best sort of powder is used; by if the gunpowder is an inferior sort, then the barrel will require the oftener washing."*

A screwdriver or "turn-screw" allowed the removal of the lock for cleaning and oiling. After rinsing the barrel with water *"as the foulness requires: when the barrel is perfectly clean, its inside must be dried by tow* (waste fibers from linen production)*, or linen rags."* If a wooden rammer was in use, friction-fitted coiled metal worms were used to affix the tow or rags unless special metal cleaning rods were available. Metal rammers (which seem to have been exceedingly rare amongst provincial issued arms) used a threaded worm fitted to the end of the rammer. To further inhibit corrosion, *"a little oil rubbed over every time of cleaning"* was then applied. Brick dust or ashes on a piece of scrap leather were used as an abrasive to polish the barrel and furniture to a bright finish.

Above
Turn-screw, c. 18th century.
Military & Historical Image Bank
www.historicalimagebank.com

Right
Worms for wooden ramrods, c. 18th century.
Recovered from the site of Fort Ticonderoga.
Collection of the Fort Ticonderoga Museum

---

[44] *A Treatise of English Shooting*, page 7 – 8.

Fowling gun by John Bumford of London, c. 1750 – 1760.
Overall length: 55 3/4", barrel length: 41", caliber: .64.
Photographed with permission from
The Colonial Williamsburg Foundation

Fowling Pieces

Shotguns used for bird hunting, also known as fowling pieces, saw limited service with Provincial regiments. These may have been brought from home or occasionally purchased outright for service. In 1758, General Abercromby's agent Hancock purchased 200 guns in Boston and noted that *"I think they are a sort will Suit, being such as our Hunters and woodsmen are fond of."*[45] Unlike military style muskets, these smooth bore arms generally lacked provisions for bayonets, sling swivels, and other military features.

---

[45] Hancock to Abercromby, May 19th, 1758. *W.O.* 34/62, as quoted in *"Mismanagement"* from the Fort Ticonderoga Bulletin, vol. XV, #4, page 261.

American Weapons of the French and Indian War

Of Sorts For Provincials

Fowling gun by Richard Wilson of London, c. 1750 – 1775.
Overall length: 63", barrel length: 47 5/8", caliber: .65.
Photographed with permission from
The Colonial Williamsburg Foundation

Light Arms

During the period when matchlock muskets, snaphaunces, and true flint locks were in use by European armies, the term "fusil" was a synonym for a flint lock musket or "fire-lock". By the middle of the eighteenth century, the term "fusil", "fuzee" or "fusee" came to be used by the English to denote a wide variety of light-weight guns. In addition to *"neat fuzees with bayonets"*, Albany merchant Rowland De Paiba also carried *"light pieces for battoemen, waggoners and Rangers."*[46] Whether intended for Indians, cavalry, infantry officers, woodsmen or waggoners, the handy size and portability of the fusil proved very popular in the American wilderness.

---
[46] *New York Mercury*, April 9th, 1759.

 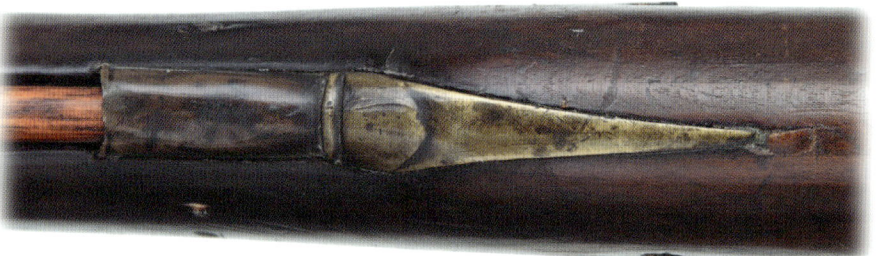

American Weapons of the French and Indian War

The stock has been wrapped to repair the cracked wrist and trigger guard.

Officer's fusil by James Barbar of London, c. 1757 – 1759. Made for the Norfolk (England) Militia.
Overall length: 52 1/2", barrel length: 37 3/16", caliber: .68.
Private collection

Fusils

Commercially manufactured, these light-weight military style arms frequently featured a slim stock, short barrel, with provision for a bayonet, sling and a smaller bore. They are often called "Officer's" fusils by modern collectors. Although heavily embellished examples were obviously intended for an upscale military market, others were not.

"...on the 9th instant in the Evening a fuzee Belonging to Capt: Aerburcrunby Were as Supposed taken by mistake as it was Lying Near His Tent Who Ever hath it are Desired to Send it To the General, it is Marked Ransford on the Lock and Made in Dublin. A Regimental Fuzee Belonging to the 44th: Marked Barbour in the Lock and Barrel Whoever has it are Desired to Return it to Lieut: Plolony."[47]

[47] *Ahearn,* page 83.

Commercial fusil or carbine bayonet, c. 1758.

American Weapons of the French and Indian War

Indian trade fusee by John Bumford of London, c. 1750 – 1760.
Overall length: 62 1/2", barrel length: 46 1/4", caliber: .59.
Photographed with permission from
The Colonial Williamsburg Foundation

Trade Fusees

Light arms intended for trade with Indians exhibited specific market driven features and decorations such as serpent sideplates, engraved motifs and at times enlarged triggerguard bows. Despite these flashy embellishments, these arms were generally of relatively low quality.

American Weapons of the French and Indian War

This fusee is fitted with sheet brass furniture.

Sir William Johnson, c. 1760.
Library and Archives Canada, Acc. No. 1989-407-1

Sir William Johnson commanded the victorious Provincial army at the battle of Lake George in 1755 as well as serving as the Northern Superintendant of Indian Affairs. In the latter capacity he oversaw the procurement and dispersal of many trade guns similar to the one shown here.

American Weapons of the French and Indian War

Traces of a stained floral design remain on the butt.

Non-Pattern Ordnance Carbine, c. 1740 – 1760.
Overall length: 42 1/8", barrel length: 25 7/8", caliber: .77.
Photographed with permission from
The Colonial Williamsburg Foundation

Ordnance storekeeper's mark.

Carbines

To further complicate matters, the term "fusil" was at times broadly used in the period for arms more appropriately termed carbines, manufactured with a side mounted sling-bar for horseback use with a broad shoulder belt featuring a spring clip. Carbines meant for horseback use sometimes mounted a bayonet, while others were stocked to the muzzle.

American Weapons of the French and Indian War

This stout carbine features an interesting, atypical mix of Sea Service and Dutch parts.

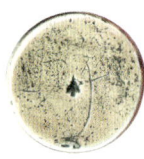  

The rammer retains the original brass tip.

American Weapons of the French and Indian War

Commercial military style musket by Watkin of Birmingham, c. 1745.
Made for the York (England) Militia.
Overall length: 57 7/8", barrel length: 41 7/8".
Photographed with permission from
The Colonial Williamsburg Foundation

Commercial Military Style Muskets

Numerous gunsmiths in England produced military-style muskets fitted with bayonets and sling swivels. At times the guns featured regulation furniture that matched current ordnance specifications. Other arms were made lighter and with cheaper, abbreviated or sheet brass hardware. The London-based firm of Richard Wilson was possibly the most prolific commercial gun maker in England during this period. Wilson manufactured a wide variety of pistols, fowlers, Indian trade fusils, military style muskets and fusees for many years. Colonies including Georgia, South Carolina, New York, and New Jersey are known to have purchased significant numbers of arms from him, making him one of the most popular manufacturers of arms for the North American trade.

View and proof marks on the breech.

Although the York muskets were not used in North America during the French and Indian War, they are excellent examples of contemporary commercial arms.

American Weapons of the French and Indian War

American composite gun, c. 1750 – 1770.
Overall length: 56 1/2", barrel length: 41", caliber: .63
Photographed with permission from
The Colonial Williamsburg Foundation

American "Composite" Muskets

Although the least glamorous variety of firearm to some, a large number of "composite" muskets saw service with provincials. Recycled English, Dutch, American, and French components from military and civilian arms were widely utilized in large numbers of repaired and restocked arms of varying quality. Arms built in America often used woods such as cherry and maple instead of the walnut and beech stocks favored by European gunsmiths.

Although some guns were restocked in the English fashion, some New England gunsmiths were heavily influenced by slender contemporary French styles. Other gunsmiths clung to the heavy club butt shapes of the century prior and some muskets from Pennsylvania and points south exhibited the characteristics of contemporary rifles.

This simple musket lacks an entry pipe.

American Weapons of the French and Indian War

This utilitarian musket lacks both a butt plate and side plate.

Of Sorts For Provincials

American rifle featuring American, French, English, and Dutch components. Date unknown. Although marked "1771", it is likely substantially earlier in manufacture.
Overall length: 58 5/16", barrel length: 43".
Wallace Gusler Collection

Rifles

"Rifle barreled guns" of the period were gaining popularity amongst back country settlers and Indians alike, but were not utilized in large numbers by any provincial forces except those of Pennsylvania and possibly Maryland. Rifles were imported and domestically produced (some with imported components). Although hampered by a slower rate of fire than a musket, the long-range accuracy of rifles won many converts on the frontier.

An interior view of the box. The wooden box cover is a modern replacement and the remains of the vent pick holder are visible.

American Weapons of the French and Indian War

The late 17th century French lock is marked "I DE PRE".

The barrel is .68 caliber and features nine groove rifling.

Note the prominent fore stock swell similar to English infantry muskets.

American Weapons of the French and Indian War

Of Sorts For Provincials

Rifle, Johanes Faber. Date unknown.
Overall length: 55 3/4", barrel length: 41 1/8".
Giles and Carolyn Cromwell collection

The wooden box cover is a modern replacement.

The cock is a period replacement.

The barrel features eight groove rifling and is .60 caliber.

American Weapons of the French and Indian War

84

Buccaneer musket, Tulle arsenal (France), c. 1740.
Overall length: 61 3/4", barrel length: 45", caliber: .75.
Robert Nittolo collection

Buccaneer Muskets

Although Buccaneer guns were typically French naval muskets favored in the Caribbean, they were in limited use in North America and some found their way into the English colonies from South Carolina to New York through capture and purchase. Some French ships were required by law to carry Buccaneer muskets to various colonial ports.[48] Buccaneer muskets featured a heavy club butt and a barrel *"of an uncommon length."*[49] These were thought by some to give these cumbersome arms increased range over shorter-barreled muskets. Official contracts stipulated barrel lengths from 48 to 60 inches with both iron and brass mounts.[50]

[48] *The Fusil de Tulle in New France*, page 19.
[49] *Captain John Knox's Journal*. July 1st, 1759, page 394.
[50] *The Fusil de Tulle in New France*, page 20.

American Weapons of the French and Indian War

American Weapons of the French and Indian War

88

Officer's Fusil by Edward North of London, c. 1750 – 1760.
Overall length: 49 3/4", barrel length: 34", caliber: .67.
Photographed with permission from
The Colonial Williamsburg Foundation

Right
Windham, William. *A plan of discipline, composed for the use of the militia of the county of Norfolk. London, 1759.* Plate 44.
Private collection

Officer's Equipment

Much like their counterparts in the Regulars, Provincial commissioned officers were generally expected to purchase their own arms, equipment and clothing. These items were frequently constructed of higher quality components and had a nicer finish than those of the enlisted men. Many Provincial officers wore clothing made of superfine wool embellished with metallic lace trim as well as gorgets, swords and sashes to differentiate them from the rank and file.

American Weapons of the French and Indian War

The metal rammer may be a working life additon.

The barrel features the maker's mark of Richard Wilson of London.

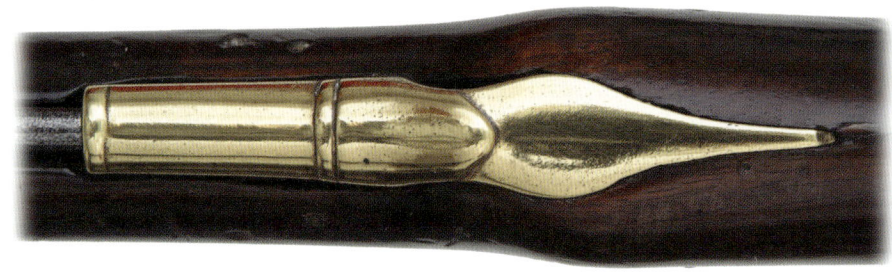

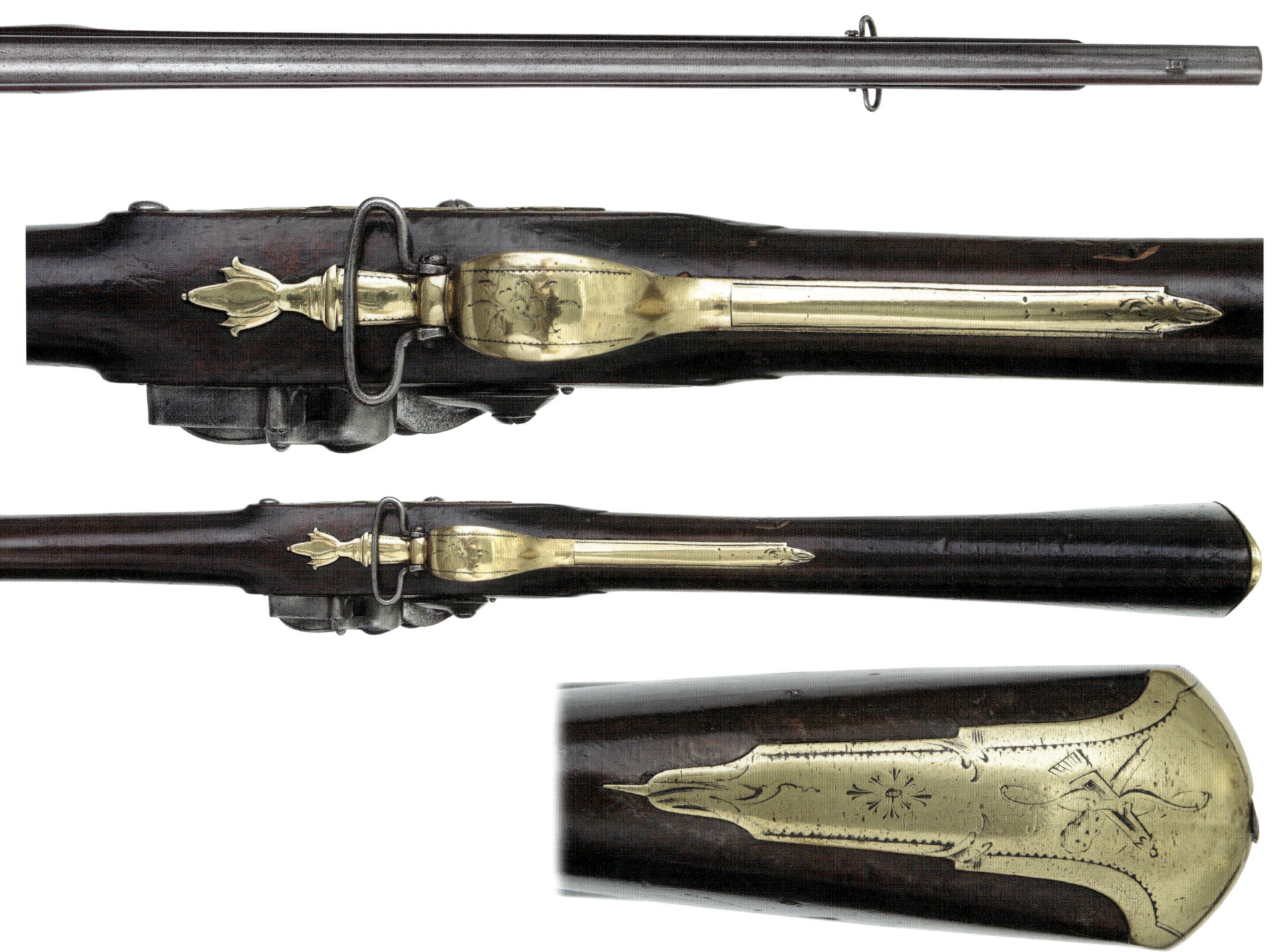

The Chamois leather backer and red silk ribbon remain intact.

Officer's gorget, c. 1750 – 1760. Photographed with permission from *The Colonial Williamsburg Foundation*

American Weapons of the French and Indian War

The side plate features a military motif.

Officer's sash, c. 18th century.
Robert Nittolo collection

Gilt-silver hilted spadroon by William Kinman of London, c. 1761.
Private collection

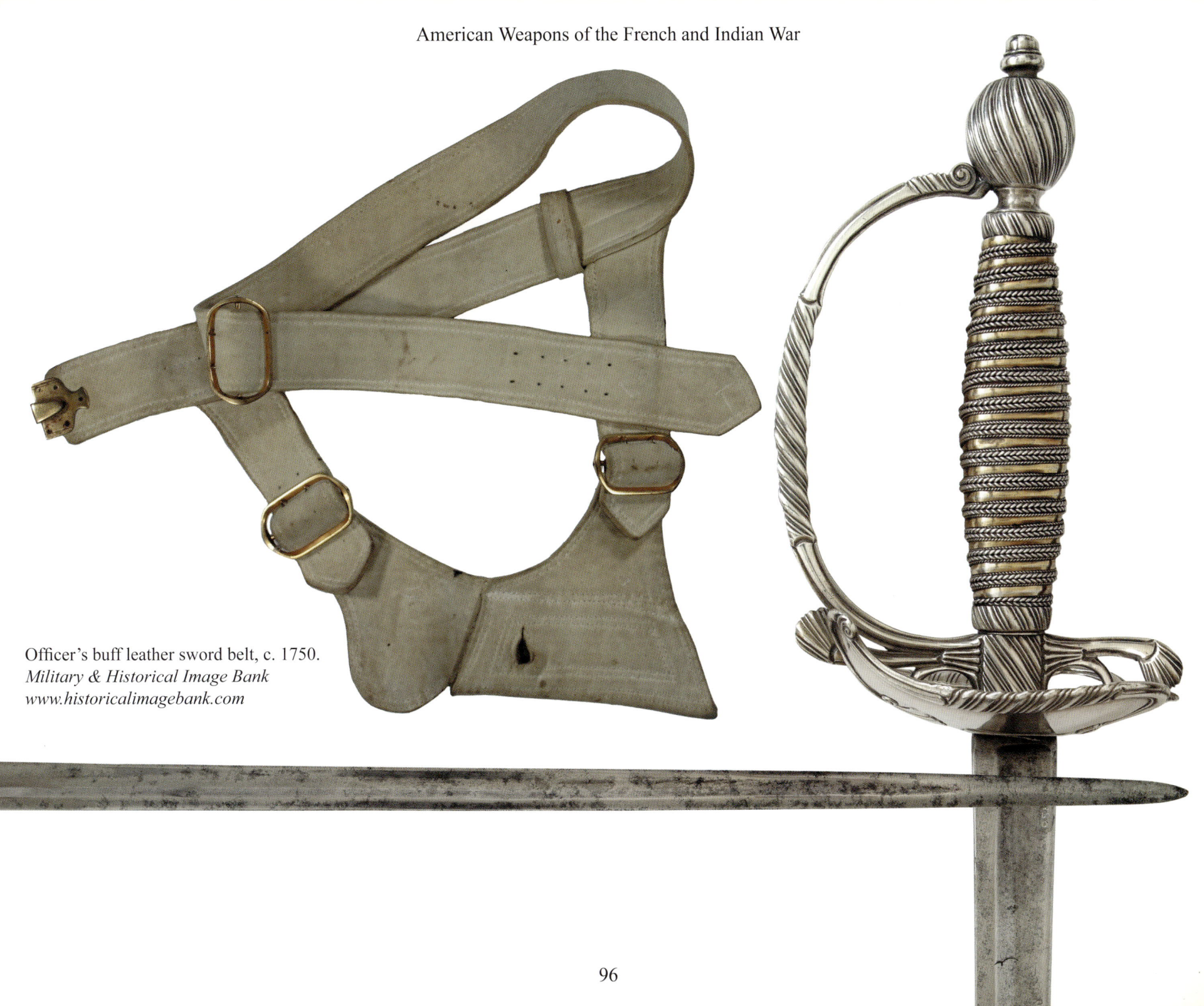

Officer's buff leather sword belt, c. 1750.
Military & Historical Image Bank
www.historicalimagebank.com

American Fowler Marked Roger Lewis, 1756.
Overall length: 70 1/2", barrel length: 54", caliber: .55.
Robert Nittolo collection

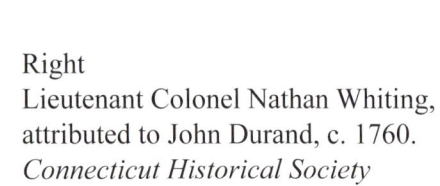

Right
Lieutenant Colonel Nathan Whiting,
attributed to John Durand, c. 1760.
Connecticut Historical Society

Connecticut

The colony of Connecticut tried several methods to supply itself with arms. On April 12, 1755, the Pennsylvania Gazette reported that *"the Governor…issued a Proclamation…for encouraging Men to enlist in his Majestys Service: By this Proclamation each able bodied Man is to have a Premium of 30s. Lawful Money, or an Equivalent in Bills of Credit; and whoever provides himself a good Firelock, Sword or Hatchet, Belt and Cartridge Box, to receive 19s. more…"* Numerous petitions desiring repayment for lost personal arms survive. John Parks complained that *"I Lost my Gun as we went to bury the Dead after the fight & I suppose Somebody took it & Carried it in as plunder from a Tree where I Sett it but I was busy in Buriing the Dead & Cant tell where it went but Conclude it was plundered."* Parks was *"A lowd £ 1.2.6"* on March 15, 1756.[51]

---

[51] *Connecticut Soldiers in the French and Indian War*, page 15.

The gun shown here belonged to and was possibly made by Roger Lewis of Farmington Connecticut, and is inscribed with his name and the date 1756. Although Roger Lewis does not appear to have served in the Connecticut Provincial forces during the French and Indian War, he did collect a pension for service in the 8th Connecticut Regiment during the Revolution. His father Josiah likely served as a Connecticut Provincial.[52] A descendant of Lewis loaned this gun for the 1885 Bristol Connecticut Centennial Celebration and the remains of the exhibition tag survive on the stock.[53]

---

[52] *Connecticut Officers and Soldiers, 1700s-1800s. "Rolls of Connecticut Men in the French and Indian War, 1755 – 1762"*. Alfred C. Bates, Vol I, p. 32, 194. Vol. II, p. 85.

[53] *Centennial Celebration of the Incorporation of the Town of Bristol*, page 84. June 17th, 1885. by J. J. Jennings Hartford, 1885.

The butt plate is marked "Roger Lewis 1756".

In February 1756, the Connecticut Assembly resolved to apply for *"at least three thousand stands of arms, with proper accoutrements…from Royal Stores"* as well as appointing *"Capt. Titus Hulburt, of New London,…to clean and fit for use the said guns, pistols and cutlashes, and also procure locks for such of said guns and pistols that have none…"*[54] Correspondence from Ordnance Comptroller James Furnis confirms that Connecticut received *"small arms & ca. delivered to them out of His Majesty's Stores"*[55] These must also be a portion of the 10,000 stands of *"Land Service Muskets of the King's Pattern with Brass Furniture, Double Bridle Locks Wood Rammers with Bayonets & Scabbards and Tann'd Leather Slings…Cartouch Boxes with Straps of 12 Holes…"*[56] received in 1756. Along with royal and personally supplied muskets, Connecticut also purchased arms on the commercial market to supply the provincials:

---

[54] *Public Records of Connecticut*, February, 1756, page 460 – 461.

[55] *Furnis Letter book*, February 9th, 1757, page 70.

[56] *W.O.* 55/412, page 3. November 12th, 1755.

Spencer Phips to Thomas Fitch
Boston 26th Febry 1757.

Sir,
The two Houses of Assembly having recd information that many of the Arms delivered to the Soldiers raised by this Government the last Year have been purchased by the Inhabitants of New York they have desired me to write to your Excellency and to desire that you would give such Orders for the recovery of them as shall appear necessary. The greater part of these Arms were King's Arms, and the remainder were new Arms lately imported at the charge of the Province, and are something lighter than the Kings Arms. I have impowered John Toye Esqr to seize & collect all he can find within this Government, and as he will pass through Connecticut in his way to Albany in Order to see if he can find any of said Arms in those parts, I would pray your Excellency's Assistance if it should be needed for the recovery of any such, which he may meet with within Your Government.

I am your Excellency's Most Obedient humble Servant
S. PHIPS.[57]

---

[57] *Fitch papers*, Volume I, page 293 – 294.

"The Gun Roll"
Captain Edmund Wells' Company, May, 1757.
Courtesy George Neumann

Identifying marks were recorded for each man's issue firelock in order to differentiate personal arms from those of the colony. *'The Gun Role"* for Captain Edmund Wells' company of Connecticut provincials, dated May 2, 1757, lists a wide variety of non-sequential fractions along with the name of the man that received each musket.

In instances where arms were lost through no fault of the men, their officers could petition that they be exempt from paying for them. On September 13, 1758, Lieutenant S. Wells certified that *"Benjamin Keeny and Clothier Prior two Privates of Colo Paysons Company were by the subscriber Commanding officer of the Party (on their Return from Fort Edward Anno 1757) ordered with the rest of ye Soldiers there to deposit their Arms in a Barn for Security and a Guard was mounted there notwithstanding which the Arms of said Keeny and Prior were Stolen away and could not be again found or heard of...NB the Number of Keenys Gun XIII/96 Number of Clothier Priors Gun 15/88..."*[58] Further arms dribbled out of Royal Stores for the Colony. A warrant signed by Jeffrey Amherst instructed Ordnance Comptroller Furnis to issue *"Arms...Connecticut 250-"* on May 28, 1759.[59]

---

[58] *Connecticut Soldiers in the French and Indian War*, page 20.
[59] *W.O.* 34/70, page 63.

American Weapons of the French and Indian War

Georgia

At the time of the French and Indian War, Georgia was a young and impoverished colony. In an ironic twist for a colony that had been run by Governor General James Oglethorpe and a regiment of regulars in the decade prior, Georgia was unable to provide itself with a provincial regiment for the duration of the war. A detachment of Virginia Provincials were in Georgia for a short time. Instead, Governor Reynolds raised troops of Rangers, which prompted Lieutenant Governor Henry Ellis to notify the board of Trade on January 1st, 1758,[60] that *"except these few Irregulars there are no forces in the Province."* In the decade prior to the French and Indian war, some military style commercial muskets were purchased from London. A report dated August 28th, 1741, indicates that the Common Council *"had order'd Mr Richard Wilson to furnish the Trust with seventy five Muskets and Bayonets of the best sort...that the ship call'd the Loyal Judith Capt. John Lemon should be hired for the voyage."*[61] General Oglethorpe's Regiment was armed with *"Land Service Musquets of the Kings Pattern with brass Furniture and Bayonets"*[62] which would indicate what are known to modern scholars as "Pattern 1730" muskets, given that this shipment predates the production of other patterns. In addition to muskets, some swords seem to have been imported during this period. A letter from the Office of Ordnance dated 27th October, 1741, mentions that *"If Mr. Oglethorpe intends the six hundred Swords for the use of the Indians, or any others than his Majestys Regular Forces, those used for Sea Service are the properest, but if they are Demanded for his Regiment, your Grace knows that this Office supplies no Regiment with Swords."*[63]

A 1753 dated guide to the Tower of London's "curiosities" states that it contained a display of *"The rising Sun, irradiated with Rays of Pistols set in a chequered*

---

[60] C.O. 5/657.

[61] *Colonial Records of the State of Georgia,* page 382.

[62] *An Account of ordnance Stores Delivered to General Oglethorpe,* October 22nd, 1741. C.O. 5/657.

[63] C.O. 5/657. page 47-48.

"Dog's Head" marine hanger, c. 1690 – 1710.
Private collection

"Dog's Head" marine hanger, c. 1690 – 1710, converted to a knife during the 18th century. Found in Georgia.
Private collection

Frame of Marine Hangers of a peculiar Make, having Brass Handles, and the Form of a Dog's Head on their Pummels."[64] Fragments of dog-headed brass hilted marine hangers have been recovered from areas with Native associations in Georgia and Alabama and specimens of that sword are still on display at the Tower. On November 19, 1756, there was an *"Order in Council for Small Arms & Ammunition to be sent to Georgia"*[65] for *"Five hundred Small arms of the Dutch Fabrick…with Bayonets and Scabbards…Cartouch Boxes with Straps of 18 Holes…"* Since all of the Dutch arms listed in Ordnance stores the year prior were listed as *"with brass Furniture"*[66] it is likely that these were of the same style as those shipped to Virginia and North Carolina in 1754, described as purchased in 1741. British officials received further correspondence from Ellis dated August 1st, 1757, *"signifying that he had received…the muskets & other particulars."*[67] In a letter from Savannah to the Board of Trade dated September 1757, Ellis wrote the following about Georgia's military efforts during the earlier stages of the war:[68]

"…tho' this Province is in a better condition at present than it has been at any time since the reduction of General Oglethorpe's Regiment- Four or Five forts of earth and Wood are built & building in different Districts, & this Town is now inclosed in the manner I described in my Last Letter- Several Small canon that were buried in the sand I have raised & mounted the greatest part on Carriages as I intend to do the rest. Lord Loudon has authorixed me to keep the Troop of Rangers on foot that Mr. Reynolds began to —[illeg.]— until his Majesty's pleasure concerning them shall be known. Besides Colo Bouquet on my application has spared us 100 of the Provincial Troops of Virginia who are quartered in this town. The Rangers have posted near the Great Indian Pass upon the Ogeachee River with orders to make themselves —[illeg.]— fully acquainted with the Country, & to raise a strong intrenchment round their camp- These are all the military dispositions our circumstances will allow us to make. The last Account we had from the Indian Countrys contain nothing unusual."

---

[64] *David Henry's Of the Tower*, page 38.

[65] *W.O. 55/412*, page 104.

[66] *State of Small Arms…in the Tower…January 14th, 1755. W.O. 47/45*, page 23 – 24.

[67] *W.O. 47/50*, page 298.

[68] *C.O. 5/646.*

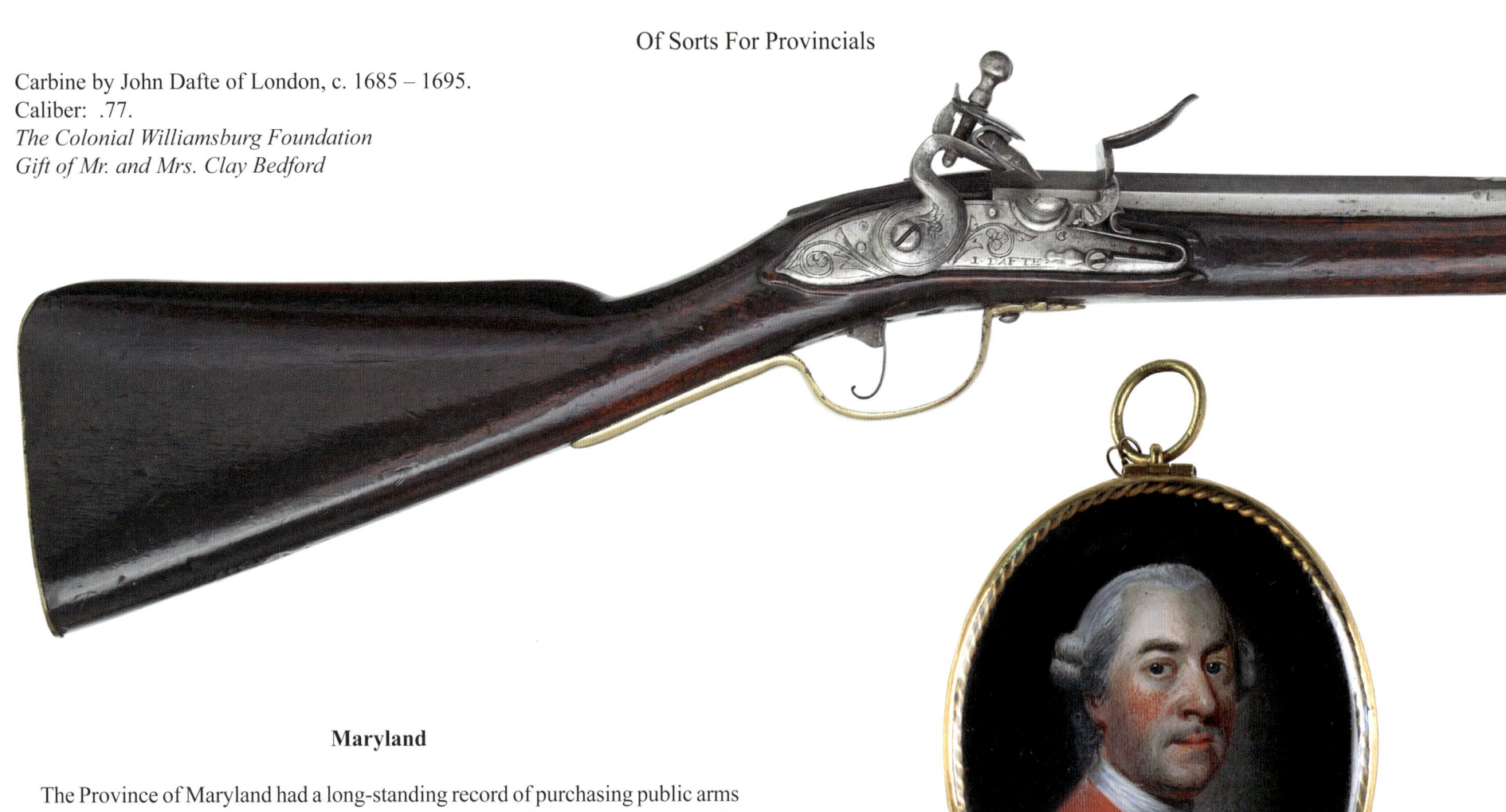

Carbine by John Dafte of London, c. 1685 – 1695.
Caliber: .77.
The Colonial Williamsburg Foundation
Gift of Mr. and Mrs. Clay Bedford

Sir John St. Clair, by John Copley, c. 1758.
As Deputy Quartermaster General, St. Clair figured prominently in arms distribution.
Courtesy of The Historical Society of Pennsylvania Collection, Atwater Kent Museum of Philadelphia

Maryland

The Province of Maryland had a long-standing record of purchasing public arms funded by a *"Duty of three Pence Sterling per Hogshead on Tobacco exported... for purchasing Arms &a."*[69] Along with powder and shot, infantry weapons including muskets and pole arms, and horseman's equipage comprised of carbines, buckets, swords, and pistols were procured by the colony. Details on the exact type of these arms are frequently lacking, although a January 7, 1697/98 purchase of *"100 fuzees"* from London were described as *"3 foot 10 inches long with round locks, wallnutt tree stocks."*[70] Given the early date of the transaction the term fuzees likely refers to full-sized muskets fitted with round-faced flintlocks and a 46-inch barrel. Arms were kept in and under the Assembly Council chamber, above the Conference Chamber, in the Repository, and in the Powder House. An armorer maintained and distributed these arms as needed.[71]

---

[69] *Maryland Assembly Proceedings*, August 5 – September 28, 1745, page 192.

[70] *Proceedings of the Council of Maryland*, 1696/7 – 98, page 365.

[71] *Maryland Assembly Proceedings*, August 5-September 28, 1745, page 78 – 79.

Prior to the French and Indian War, the Maryland assembly concluded that it would be *"impossible…without making Use of those now in the Province purchased by the Publick, and which Use We think the more proper as the Expedition tends in the highest Degree to the safety of this Province."* in order to comply with the *"Royal Commands"* for arming the expedition to *"reduce Canada"* in 1746.[72] Arms were *"delivered out of the Public Magazine there"* and upon repeated applications by the Governor, Lord Calvert, *"Three hundred Musquets with Slings and bayonets, Three hundred Cartouch boxes with belts, Six Drums, Nine Half Pikes and Six Halberts"* were ordered to be replaced free of charge by a Royal Warrant dated June 1st, 1753.[73] As war broke in North America, an arms inventory was ordered, *"read and assented to, and signed, by Order of the House, by the Honourable Speaker; and was sent to the Upper House, by Mr. Charles Goldsborough and Major Travers."*[74]

Mr. J. J. Mackall brings in, and delivers to Mr. Speaker, the following Report, viz.

By the Committee appointed to inspect the Arms and Ammunition, and Accounts relating thereto, May 29, 1754. Your Committee having inspected the Arms and Ammunition, in the City of Annapolis, do find the same as follows, viz.

In the Council Chamber, 261 Muskets, well cleaned, but many of the Locks out of Order, 131 Carbines, 71 Pistols, 20 Trumpets, 7 Drums, 74 Swords, 44 Cartouch Boxes and Belts, 10 old Ditto with-out Belts, 49 Halberds and Pikes, 46 Buckets and Slings, 50 Sword Blades, 18 Daggers, and 12 Carbine Bayonets.

---

[72] *Maryland Assembly Proceedings*, June 17 – July 8, 1746, page 286.

[73] W.O. 55/411, page 72.

[74] *Proceedings and Acts of the Maryland General Assembly*, page 456. online source: http://www.mdarchives.state.md.us/megafile/msa/speccol/sc2900/sc2908/000001/000050/html/am50--511.html

In the Room over the Conference Chamber, 72 old Muskets and Carbines much out of Repair, 33 Pair of Holsters, 155 Swords, 25 Bayonets, 75 Sword Belts, 16 old Cutlasses, 6 new Drums, 34 Pistols well cleaned, but the Locks much out of Order, 3 Chests and a half of Match, 15 Pair of Drum Sticks: Also the following new Arms, viz. 12 Brass Trumpets with Brass Mouth Pieces, 12 Drums and Sticks compleat, 19 Carbines with Buff Slings, Bayonet Cases, and 7 Bayonets, 19 Muskets, and 30 Bayonet Cases.

We also find, that in July, 1751, there was delivered out to Doctor Steuart, by the Order of Samuel Ogle, Esq; then Governor, as appears by said Steuart's Receipt, 11 new Carbines, 11 Buff Slings, 11 Bayonets, and 11 Scabbards, which are not since returned. As also the following new Arms, imported in the Ship Sally, William Anderson Contractor, and Patrick White Master, viz. Muskets, Slings, and Bayonets, 300 each, in 12 Chests, Cartouch Boxes with Straps 300, Scabbards for Bayonets 300, Drums compleat 6, in 3 Cases, 9 Half Pikes, and Six Halberds. The new Guns, to Appearance, seem to be very good, and that some of them at the Top of the Chests are cleaned, but the greater Part are in very bad Order, and for Want of cleaning, are much rustied.

In the Room under the Conference Chamber, 2700 lbs. of Ball, 300 lbs. of large Shot, 980 lbs. of Bar Lead. In the Powder House, 134 Sword Belts, 42 Carbine Slings, half a Box of Flints, 20 half Barrels of new Powder, 8 half Barrels and in The Lower House. 511 whole Barrel of old Ditto, no Kegs of Shot, and 2 half Barrels of Ditto. There are 10 old Guns lying on the Point, near Mr. Patrick Creagh's Warehouse, not fit for Use, and 15 new Ditto without Carriages, much rustied, and will, in all Probability, be much damaged, if not speedily prevented.

All which is humbly submitted to your Honourable House.

Signed per Order, Benjamin Beall, Clerk. Which was read, and Ordered, that the Committee of Laws do prepare an Address to his Excellency, requesting him to remove the present Armourer, and to appoint some able Person to act in the said Office, and to request his Excellency to dispose of the Money raised for Arms, to purchase Arms to be distributed on the Frontiers of this Province. Doctor Carroll, from the Committee of Laws, brings in, and delivers to Mr. Speaker an Address to his Excellency; which was read, approved, and ordered to be ingrossed.

Signed p Order M Macnemara Cl: Lo: Ho.

This inventory indicates a wide variety of arms of mixed vintage and in varied stages of repair as the *"Committee Beg leave to Inform you that the fire locks and pistols in General are unfit for service owing Intirely to the Neglect and Incapacity of the Armourer."*[75] Two companies of provincials were then ordered to be raised by Governor Sharpe and were to receive *"Cloaths, Arms and Accoutrements."*[76] A total of *"one hundred and five new Arms to Capt. Dagwortys Company with slings Cartouch Boxes and Bayonets"* were issued out of stores on June 14, 1754.[77] A company of 53 Maryland provincials commanded by Captain Dagworthy took part in the Braddock expedition, and were at Will's Creek on June 8, 1755.[78] In addition to public arms and the replacement arms from the Tower, additional carbines were being bought privately following the disastrous Braddock campaign.

August 21, 1755 The Pennsylvania Gazette ANNAPOLIS, August 7.

We hear, that the Inhabitants of Baltimore Town have purchased, by Subscription, a Quantity of Carbines, Bayonets, and Cartouch Boxes, which are to be preserved in a publick Repository, for the Defence of that flourishing Place.

---

[75] *Maryland Assembly Proceedings*, Feb. 23 – May 22, 1756, page 318.
[76] *Pennsylvania Gazette*, August 18th, 1754, Item #17282.
[77] *Maryland Assembly Proceedings*, Feb. 23 – May 22, 1756, page 318.
[78] A Return of the Virginia, Mary-Land & North Carolina Troops, Encamp'd at Will's Creek-June the 8th, 1755. *Military Affairs in North America*, edited by Pargellis, page 88-89.

American Weapons of the French and Indian War

Commercial Carbine by Ludlam, c. 1750.
Overall length: 47 5/8", barrel length: 32", caliber: .68.
Photographed with permission from
The Colonial Williamsburg Foundation

On April 24, 1756, Massachusetts Governor Shirley (who was then acting commander in Chief in North America) wrote Maryland's Governor Sharpe that he was to receive *"300 Stands with a proper proportion of Ammunition…to return the Arms at the End of the present Service, for wch they are lent to the province."*[79] These arms would have been a portion of the 10,000 Long Land muskets with wooden rammers sent to Shirley in the winter of 1755. In addition, Maryland received replacement (possibly Dutch) arms from North Carolina to replace arms loaned the year prior:

> *There were 150 Muskets sent hence to the Carolina Troops the Summer before last: Col. Innes, as appears by the Armourer's Account, has returned only 132, but 28 of them have Bayonets, and are much better than what he borrowed.*[80]

The arms of two deserters from the Maryland Forces stationed at Fort Frederick were described in the Maryland Gazette — William Withers *"carried off with him a Gun that appeared on the out Side of the Barrel like a Rifle, but was smooth bored"* and John Hawkins *"carried off with him a Carbine and Rifle."* The well-armed deserters likely intended to sell these arms, and the advertisement reminded the reader that *"any Person who may conceal or entertain them, or purchase their Arms, will be punished as the Law Directs."*[81]

---

[79] Shirley to Sharpe, April 24th, 1756. *Correspondence of Governor Sharpe*, page 392.
[80] *Maryland Assembly Proceedings*, Feb. 23 – May 22, 1756.
[81] *Maryland Gazette*, August 12th, 1756.

Possibly the mark of William Staples.

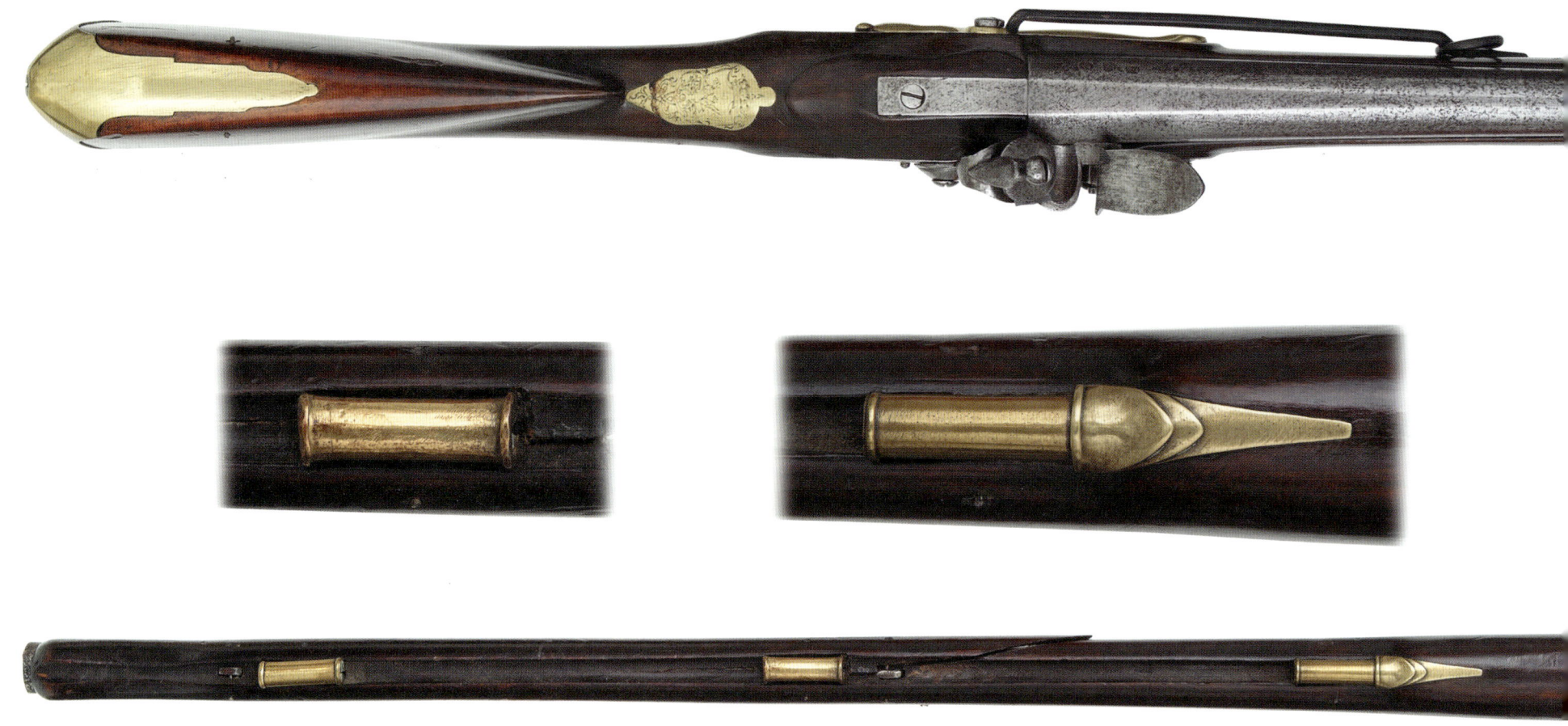

Maryland later contributed arms to the Forbes expedition. Governor Sharpe wrote General Forbes that *"500 new muskets...have been since sent... to Winchester to arm the Virginia Forces..."*[82] in addition to the cavalry carbines, swords, and pistols supplied for the Virginia Light Horse in 1758.

Given the descriptions of arms in stores, both Maryland provincials and militia seem to have fielded with an incredibly mixed lot of muskets and carbines. A report from the Maryland Assembly dated April 13, 1762 indicates that *"Firelocks, short Muskets and Carbines"* were all returned from *"Coll. Dagworthy's Company."* Maryland's participation in the war came to a close, a final wartime tally of arms was taken:

April 13, 1762

Your Committee having inspected the Arms and Ammunitions in the City of Annapolis do find that there is in the possession of the Armourer the following Arms and Ammunition vizt. Your Committee find that since the last Report of the State of the Arms and Ammunition, there have been received by the Armourer into the Magazine from Mr. James Dick [a Maryland merchant] *21 chests of Arms*

---

[82] Sharpe to Forbes, June 9th, 1758. *Forbes Papers, Box,* #4.

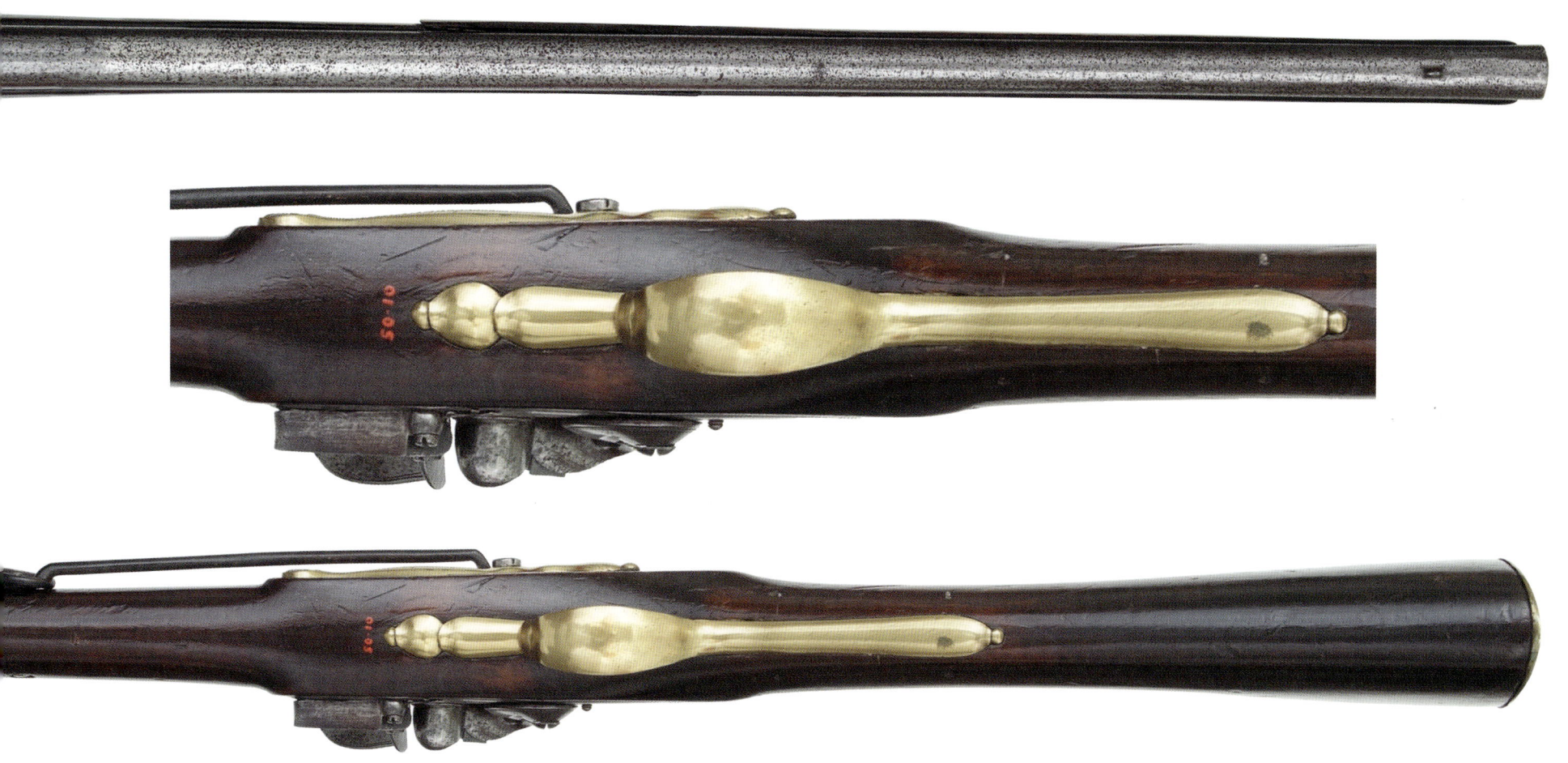

containing 500 Muskets, Bayonets, Slings, Cartouch Boxes and Bullett Moulds, and that there have been returned from Coll. Dagworthy's Company. 86 Firelocks, short Muskets and Carbines, 18 Cartouch Boxes, 10 old Slings, 8 hair Pouches and Powder Horns. And your committee also find that out of the Arms and Ammunitions mentioned in said last Report to be in the Magazine the arms since returned and those since imported and delivered to the Armourer. He has delivered out by the Governour's Order, the several Arms and Quantities of Ammunition mentioned in the following Copy of his Account for which he produced Vouchers to your Committee, Vizt.

By order of his Excellency Horatio Sharpe Esqr. Lieutenant General, and Governor and Commander in Chief in and over the Province of Maryland and Avalon, delivered out of the Magazine and Stores of the City of Annapolis.

American "hair pouch". Date unknown.
Eight hair pouches were returned to stores by
Dagworthy's Company in 1762.
Photographed with permission from
The Colonial Williamsburg Foundation

American Weapons of the French and Indian War

The sling bar allowed the horseman to suspend the carbine from a broad shoulder belt while mounted.

American restocked musket, c. 1750 – 1760, from parts c. 1700 – 1710.
Overall length: 62 1/2", barrel length: 46".
Robert Nittolo collection

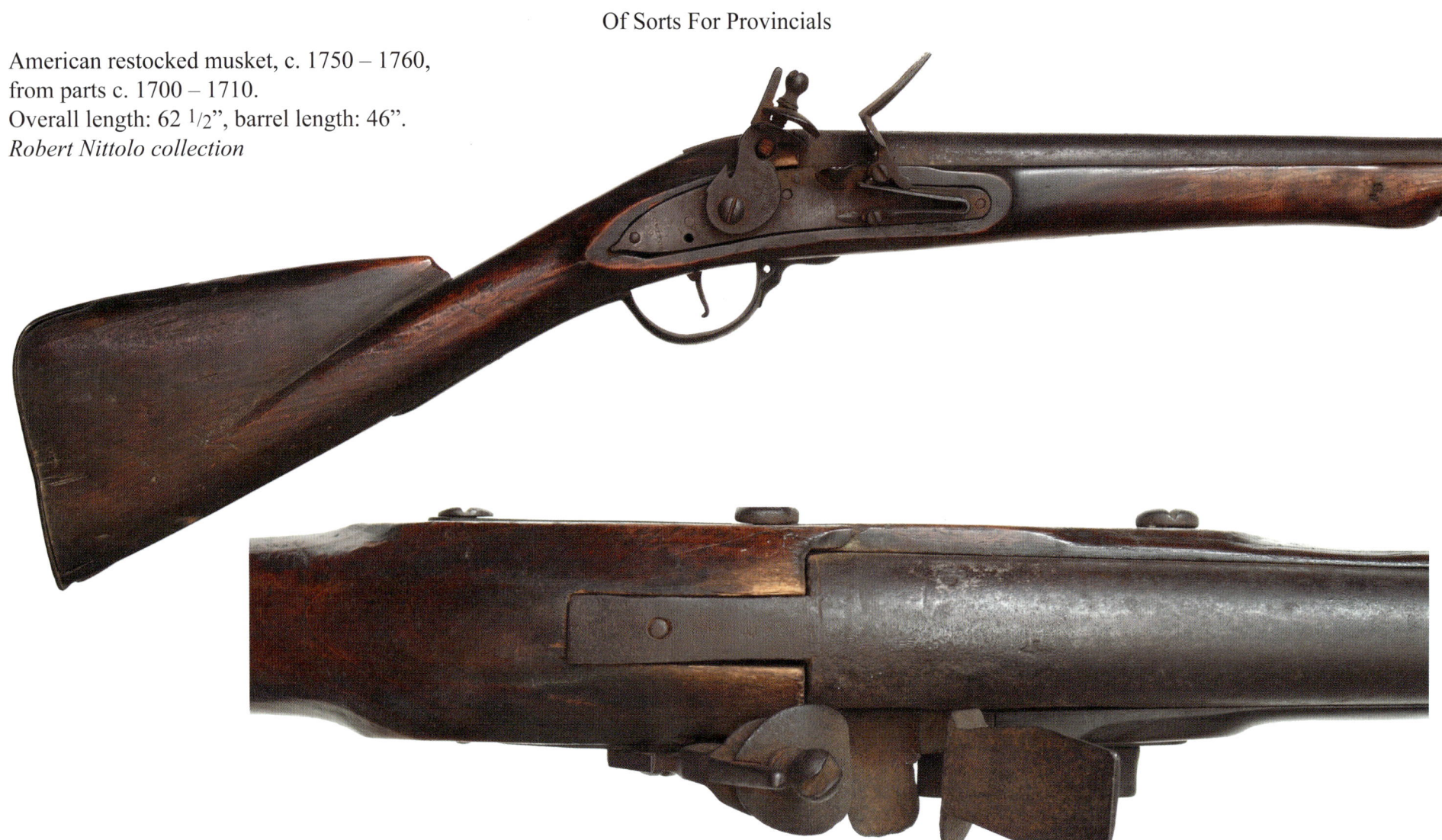

Massachusetts

Archaeological evidence from Fort Frederick, in modern-day Pemaquid, Maine (circa 1729 to 1759) indicates that the Massachusetts men there were at least partially armed with dog lock muskets likely manufactured in the first quarter of the eighteenth century.[83] Portions of an English flat-bladed socket bayonet of similar vintage were also recovered from the same site.[84] A fragmentary brass sideplate from the fort in what was formerly part of the Massachusetts Colony closely mirrors those of other dog lock muskets manufactured from 1708 to 1710.[85]

In order to supply the force sent against Nova Scotia's Chignecto Isthmus and the French fort at Beausejour in the spring of 1755, Governor William Shirley received 2,000 *"Land Muskets of the King's Pattern."*[86] Shirley later noted that *"the 2000 stands of Arms consign'd to me the last Spring were all distributed among the 2000 New England Men sent to Nova Scotia."*[87]

---

[83] *The Forts of Pemaquid, Maine*, pages 74 – 75.

[84] *Ibid.*, page 83.

[85] *Battle Weapons*, page 53 – 54.

[86] October 13th, 1755. *W.O.* 55/411, page 77.

[87] Shirley to Robinson, September 28th, 1755. *PRO CO* 5/46. *Correspondence of Shirley*, page 298.

The lock is engraved "Boulton 9".

The two Massachusetts provincial battalions commanded by Colonel John Winslow and Lieutenant Colonel George Scott each numbered 1,000 men. Ordnance Comptroller Furnis wrote the Board on July 16, 1756 that these arms were returned, although now only numbering *"1166...from General Winslows and Lt Colonel Scott's Provincials, most of which are in a very bad Condition..."*[88]

Along with the attack on Nova Scotia, plans were developed for another campaign against Crown Point. The *"List of articles provided and providing by the Committee of War in Massachusetts for Crown Point Expedition"* (from a Report dated June 7, 1755) lists amongst numerous other items:

400 small arms
1200 cartouch boxes
1500 Powder flasks
1300 Powder horns
1500 worms & 1500 wires
1500 knapsacks & bullet pouches[89]

---

[88] *W.O.* 47/48, page 272.
[89] *Provincial Papers...of New Hampshire,* page 396.

English flat bladed bayonet, c. 1700 – 1720.
Recovered from the vicinity of Fort Ticonderoga.
Private collection

English flat bladed bayonet, c. 1700 – 1720.
Private collection

When Massachusetts provincials Solomon Raines and Harper Wainset deserted *"Captain Thomas William's Company of Colonel Fitch's Regiment"*, they carried off a *"Firelock, [marked] NO. XVIII, and branded on the Britch N.Y."*[90]

Massachusetts must have received a portion of the 10,000 stands of *"Land Service Muskets of the King's Pattern with Brass Furniture, Double Bridle Locks Wood Rammers with Bayonets &Scabbards and Tann'd Leather Slings…Cartouch Boxes with Straps of 12 Holes…"*[91] As elsewhere, returning the arms at the conclusion of the campaign proved to be problematic. In an entry dated 7 March, 1757, Comptroller Furnis indicates that *"out of the 2,000 issued to the Province of the Massachusetts Bay, he has just yet received 300 only…"*[92]

Impressment was another source of arms for the provincial soldiers of Massachusetts. John Norton *"of Edgartown…Dukes-County"* petitioned the Massachusetts House of Representatives *"shewing that he impressed sundry Guns for Men who inlisted into his Majesty's Service for the Crown-Point Expedition in 1755, which have not been returned to their Owners."*[93] On June 11, 1756, Jacob Fowle requested reimbursement for *"fire arms"* that had been impressed *"in order to Compleat the 2000 Men Ordered to be raised…"*[94]

Arms were also purchased privately. Massachusetts' Governor Pownall bought over 1,450 firearms in Boston in April and May of 1758 during the chaotic arms shortfall of that year.[95] This prompted Governor Pownall to reroute the march of some newly recruited men as the provincials were *"extreamly uneasy about going thro' the Woods without Arms…"*[96]

---

[90] *New York Gazette, or Weekly Post Boy*, August 30th, 1756.
[91] *W.O. 55/412*, page 3. Nov. 12th, 1755.
[92] *Furnis Letterbook*, page 81.
[93] *Journals of the House of Representatives of Massachusetts*, Volume XXXIII, part 2, page 314 – 315.
[94] *Massachusetts Archives Collection*, Volume 303, page 077C – 077D.
[95] *John Cardwell's Mismanagement*, page 261.
[96] *Ibid.*, page 265.

Further complicating matters, some provincial officers allowed their men to return home when arms and supplies did not arrive in camp in a timely fashion. Colonel Thomas Doty was singled out in a scathing article in the Boston Post Boy for allowing his men *"to quit the Service and return Home."* Doty's claim that *"he cou'd not supply them with Blankets, Haversacks, Canteens, Hatchets and Arms, as had been promised by the Government"* was refuted by the paper which published an *"Account of Warlike Stores deliver'd Col., Thomas Doty's Regiment"* including three shipments in May of 1758 totaling *"220 Arms, 207 Bayonets, 6 Cartouch boxes, 230 Slings, 1000 Blankets, 1000 Knapsacks, 1000 Flasks, 183 Tin Kettles…"* The article further noted that *"This was the Proportion of Province Arms deliver'd to each Regiment, besides what private Arms each Company had before they March'd, and besides Four Hundred and Ten Arms sent by His EXCELLENCY."*[97]

At least one blacksmith sought to cash-in on the shortage of proper arms by offering to produce bayonets for the provincials. Jonathan Dakin *"at the Blue Ball, near the Mill Bridge in Boston…"* advertised that he would *"undertake to supply the Province with Bayonets, to be made Workman like, and of good Stuff; without which he knows they will no Ways answer the End for which they are to be made…"*[98] Further illustrating the chaos is a petition of *"Samuel Smith Capt. Of the Military Foot Company"* dated October 10 1758. Smith related that he had contracted with a local Blacksmith to provide him with bayonets; although *"The Bayonets appeared well & handsomely made and the Smith demands Six Shillings for each of them"*, the arrangement produced only six bayonets as *"the guns being of different Sizes the Smith grew discouraged in proceeding to make more."*[99]

---

[97] August 7th, 1758. Printed by J. Green, and J. Russell, Queen Street, Boston.
[98] *Boston Gazette*, February 6th, 1758.
[99] *Massachusetts Archives Collection*, Volume 303, page 085 – 085A.

Moses Marcy in a Landscape, c. 1755.
Oil on wood overmantel panel from the
Moses Marcy House, Southbridge, MA.
Accession No. 20.19.1
Henry Peach, photographer
Courtesy Old Sturbridge Village, MA

Personal arms were repeatedly encouraged for recruits. This practice seems to have been most prevalent in the colonies of New England. Some of the firearms that went on the Crown Point Expedition with Massachusetts men in 1755 were privately owned. Governor Pownall issued a proclamation which was printed in the Boston Gazette on March 26, 1759, that stated *"as most People in North America have Arms of their own, which from their being accustomed to and being so much lighter than the Tower-Arms, must be more agreeable and proper for them, General Amherst, as an Encouragement for their coming provided with good Muskets, engages to pay for every one they shall so bring that may be spoiled or lost in actual Service at the Rate of Twenty-Five-Shillings Sterling."*

Jonathan Barnard *"of Waltham, in the County of Middlesex"* petitioned the Massachusetts House of Representatives to be reimbursed for the value of a personal firearm lost when his unnamed son was *"killed in the Battle near Lake-George."*[100] In 1760, Ruth Farmer petitioned for the value of her dead husband's gun. William Farmer *"Inlisted himself into ye Governments service in ye Canada Expedition in ye year 1758 under ye Command of Capt. Salmon Whitney in ye Regiment of Collo. Bagley"* and was killed *"in ye Batle at ye fight at Tiaconderoga."* Ruth was *"...left with four young children with neither house nor Land."* The widowed Farmer was awarded 40 shillings for her husband's gun.[101]

---

[100] *Journals of the House of Representatives of Massachusetts*, Volume XXXIV, part 2, page 253.
[101] *Fort Ticonderoga Bulletin*, Volume 2, #2. July, 1930, page 79.

Excavated side plate, c. 1700 – 1720.
Shown actual size.
Private collection

A military-style musket made by Wilson with a Massachusetts provenance survives. It is marked with the name Joshua Holt, 1756. Holt served as a Massachusetts provincial through the course of the war and was promoted to ensign in 1762. His musket is very similar to examples from New York and New Jersey with the addition of an improvised wrist escutcheon and his personal markings. It is unknown whether originally a personally-owned firearm or a part of a bulk commercial purchase by the colony.

An obviously frustrated Governor Pownall addressed the Massachusetts House of Representatives on January 6, 1759: *"I Had caused about three Thousand Stand of Arms to be delivered to the Men, raised the last Year for His Majesty's Service, under General Abercromby; I have an Account of one Hundred and fifteen only, as yet returned."*[102] Due to such shortfalls, personal arms and those owned by the colony continued to be augmented by those from Royal Stores for the 1759 campaign. A warrant signed by Jeffrey Amherst instructed Ordnance Comptroller Furnis to issue *"Arms…Massachusetts 125"* on 28 May, 1759.[103]

---

[102] *Message from the Governor Journals of the House of Representatives of Massachusetts*, Volume XXXV, page 140.
[103] *W.O. 34/70*, page 63.

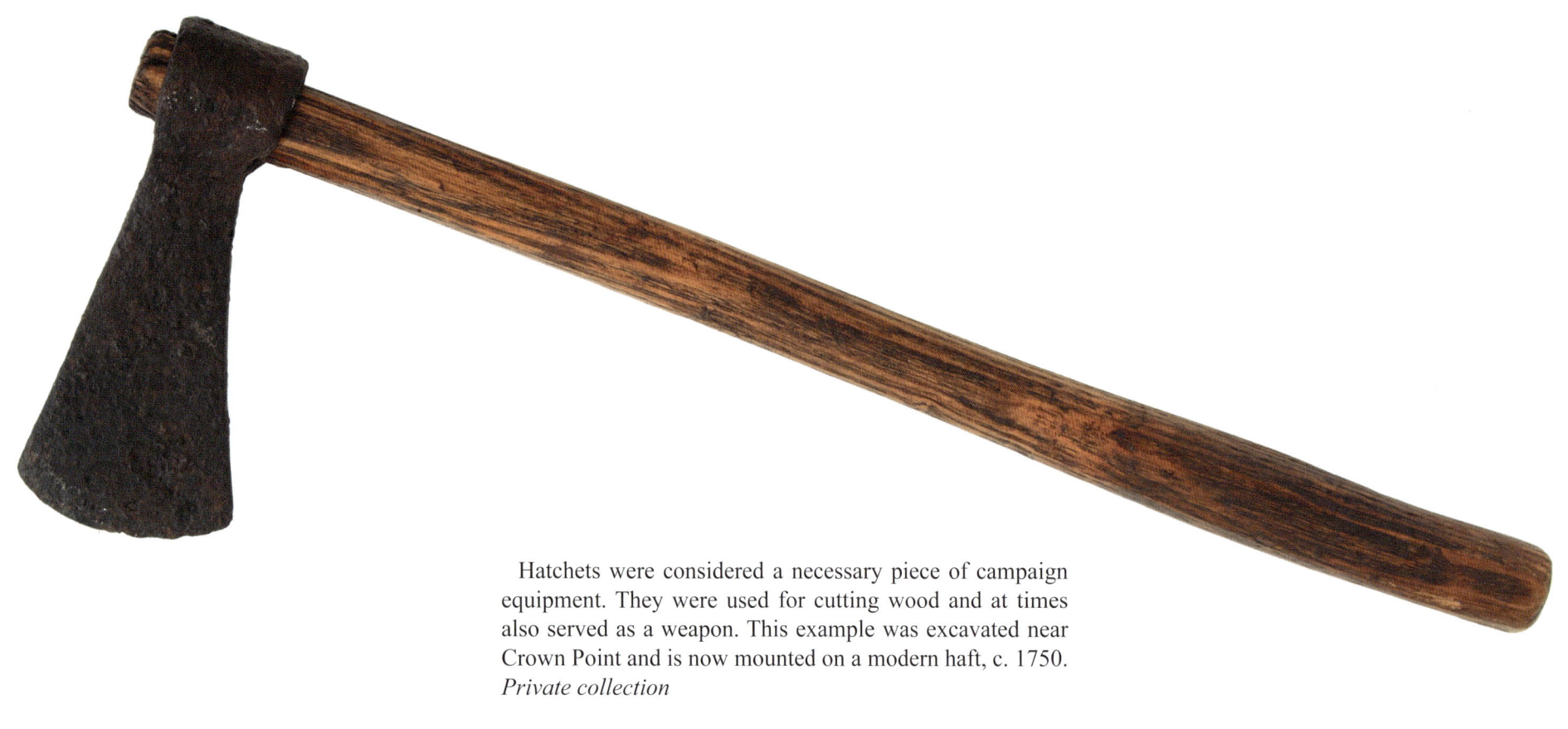

Hatchets were considered a necessary piece of campaign equipment. They were used for cutting wood and at times also served as a weapon. This example was excavated near Crown Point and is now mounted on a modern haft, c. 1750. *Private collection*

New Hampshire

New Hampshire, like the other New England colonies, faced arms shortages in the opening stages of the war. Ordnance Comptroller James Furnis' letter book indicates that the *"Provinces of Massachusetts Bay, Connecticut, Rhode Island, and New Hampshire"* received *"small arms & ca. delivered to them out of His Majesty's Stores."*[104] Here too we find some of the 10,000 stands of *"Land Service Muskets of the King's Pattern..."*[105] received for the 1756 campaign.

Scarcity forced New Hampshire to follow a similar path to it's neighbors by offering a bounty and guarantee for the personal arms of enlistees. William Clifford petitioned the New Hampshire Committee of war in March, 1757 as *"he had a Son in the Late Regiment in Capt Winslows Company whos name was Benja Clifford and that he Died thear & that his Gun was returned into the Store which Gun was Worth Twenty five Pounds."*[106] In addition to the gun, the elder Clifford petitioned for recompense for his son's *"Kenduce [Cartouch or Cartridge] box...one pair of Buckels [buckles]...one hanchife [handkerchief]...one hatchet..."*[107]

---

[104] *Furnis Letter book*, February 9th, 1757, page 70.
[105] *W.O.* 55/412, page 3. Nov. 12th, 1755.
[106] *The State of New Hampshire: Miscellaneous Provincial Papers*, Volume XVIII, page 451 - 452.
[107] *Ibid.*

Contract musket by Richard Wilson of London, c. 1755.
Recovered from Sabbath Day Point, NY.
Robert Nittolo collection

New Jersey

Like many neighboring colonies, New Jersey's provincial "Blues" (a name likely derived from the blue uniforms worn in earlier campaigns) found themselves ill-prepared for the French and Indian War. A flurry of activity occurred as attempts were made to organize for the coming conflict. Legislation passed on April 23, 1755 stipulated that:

"*the Property of all the coulours, Drums, Halberts and Stands of Arms, Tents, Stores and other Necessaries therunto appertaining, as shall be purchased by, or given to this Colony, is hereby declared to be vested in the Colony of New-Jersey: And that they shall before they are delivered to the Soldiers to be raised for the Expedtion, be branded or mark'd with the Words New-Jersey, and Number'd; which said Brand or Mark, shall at all Times be Evidence of their being the property of the said Colony. And it shall and may be lawful for the Paymaster of the Forces of this Colony, and he is hereby directed to retain in his Hands, one forth Part of the Pay of each Soldier, to lay n his Hands as a Security for the Return of all such Stands of Arms and Accoutrements, as shall not be lost or destroyed by*

Commercial musket by Richard Wilson of London, c. 1750 – 1760.
Overall length: 61", barrel length: 46", caliber: .75.
Robert Nittolo collection

unavoidable Accident. And at the End of said Expedition, he shall receive such Stands of Arms and Accoutrements from the Soldiers for the Use of this Colony, and then to pay off the Arrears of such Soldier returning his Arms and Accoutrements in good order, or to such as shall have their Arms and Accoutrements lost or destroyed, and adjudged by a Board of Officers to have been done by unavoidable Accident; and deliver such Stands of Arms, Colours, Drums, Halberts, Tents and Stores, to the Treasurer of the Eastern Division of this Colony, to be safely kept for the Use of this Colony, until some further Provision shall be made for disposing of the same."

This same legislation also allowed a refund of *"Seven Shillings and Six–pence"* for those who enlisted with their own *"good sufficient Firelock"* but lost or destroyed it while in the service of the colony.[108] Several examples of New Jersey-marked commercial arms by Wilson survive, and runaway servant Jacob Holler carried off *"a Gun, Bayonet and Cartridge Box, the Gun and Cartridge Box…marked NEW JERSEY on them."*[109] The order for marking the arms seems to have been carried out on a widespread basis.

In May of 1755, Virginia's Lieutenant Governor Robert Dinwiddie was ordered by General Braddock to loan quantities of Dutch Arms that had recently been imported into Virginia to New Jersey and New York.

---

[108] New Jersey Province Session Laws, April 7 – 26, 1755. Printed by Bradford in Philadelphia; *New Jersey State Library Collections*.

[109] *The Pennsylvania Gazette*, June 6th, 1765.

The butt plate is engraved "New Jersey".

In a letter to the Earl of Halifax, Lt. Governor Dinwiddie wrote that Virginia's stores of arms were then quite lacking as *"we have few Guns and little Amunit'n in our Magazine, hav'g sent 1,200 Arms to N. York and the Jerseys to qualify them to execute the Plan ag'st Crown Point and Niagara."*[110] The arms invoice for New Jersey does not survive among Dinwiddie's papers, but the quantities for the New York shipments are known and show that New Jersey most likely received 500 stands of muskets of "Dutch Fabrick."

Although desperately needed, the arms garnered complaints: *"...the Arms sent the last Year to the Govr. Of Virginia, part of which he lent to the provincial Troops of New York and New Jerseys, are equally bad; insomuch, that the general bad Character, which at present prevails by this means in the Colonies, of his Majesty's Arms, will, besides the other ill Consequences, which may arise to his Troops in Action, prejudice his Service here, if not rectify'd."*[111]

---

[110] Dinwiddie to the Earl of Halifax, August 7th, 1755. *Dinwiddie papers*, page 141 – 142.
[111] William Shirley to Sir Thomas Robinson, September 28th, 1755. PRO CO 5/46.

Following the campaign of 1755, the government of New Jersey complained to Royal officials that it had *"No Fortification or Place of Defence in the Province, nor any Cannon Small Arms or Military Stores belonging thereto."*[112] By the summer of 1757, some New Jersey provincials were armed with Richard Wilson's commercial military-style muskets. Multiple relics of Wilson's manufacture have been recovered from the site of the bloody defeat of Jersey men at Sabbath Day Point, New York. All of the arms retain their New Jersey markings on their distinctive Wilson butt plates.

Legislation passed in the fall of 1757 provided funding for *"the Two Thousand Stand of Arms sent for the Use of the Province."*[113] In addition to muskets, fragments of wooden blocks from shoulder slung cartridge pouches with 23 holes have been recovered from the Sabbath Day Point site.[114] Possible New Jersey Provincial usage of the more expensive pouches associated with British regulars is not unreasonable. Commercial purchases were not sufficient to supply New Jersey for the duration of the war. A warrant signed by Jeffrey Amherst instructed Ordnance Comptroller Furnis to issue *"Arms…New Jersey…108"* on 28 May, 1759.[115]

---

[112] List of Applications for Stores & CA Defending Before the Committee. May, 1756; *Military Affairs in North America*, page 168 – 169.

[113] New Jersey Province Session Laws, October 12 – November 20, 1757. Printed by Parker in Woodbridge; *New Jersey State Library Collections*.

[114] *Collector's Illustrated Encyclopedia of the American Revolution*, page 71 #26.

[115] *W.O.* 34/70, page 63.

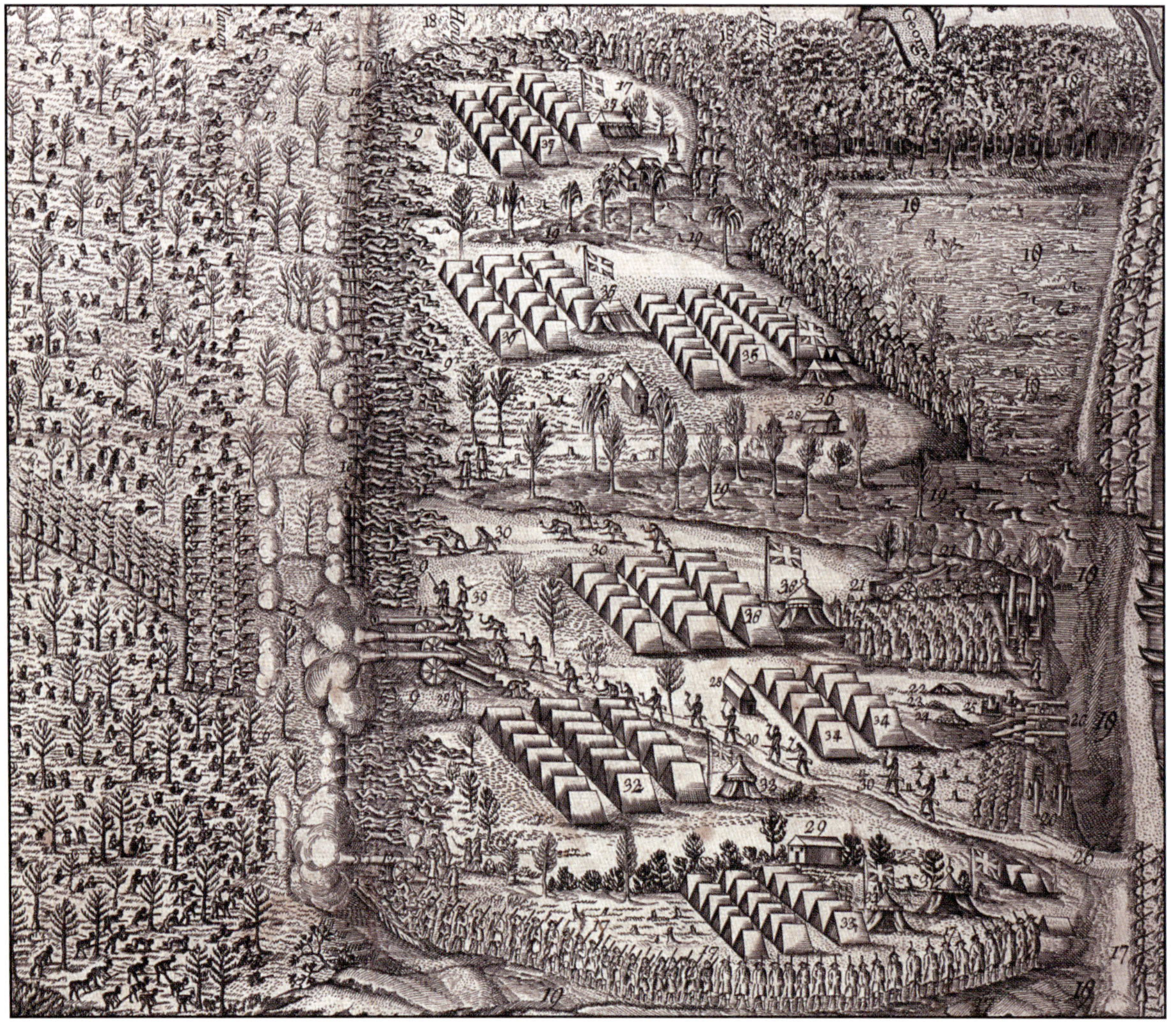

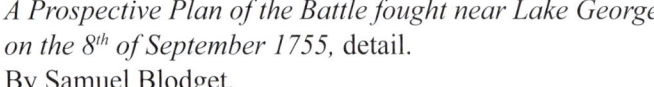
A Prospective Plan of the Battle fought near Lake George on the 8th of September 1755, detail.
By Samuel Blodget.
Courtesy The Colonial Williamsburg Foundation

American Weapons of the French and Indian War

Left
Cartidge pouch, c. 1750 – 1770.
Archeological evidence from Sabbath Day Point indicates that New Jersey Provinicals may have been equipped with cartridge pouches of this type.
Military & Historical Image Bank
www.historicalimagebank.com

New York

In May of 1755, New York received Dutch muskets originally imported into Virginia in order *"to qualify them to execute the Plan ag'st Crown Point and Niagara."*[116] These were sent to the Secretary of New York, William Alexander, via the *"Sloop John, Sam'l Tingle, Com'd'r, 500 Small Arms, with Slings, Cartouch Boxes and Bayonets, 10 Drums and 15 Halberts, shipped on the Risque of the Colony of New Jersey; they are the same sort of Arms our forces have, and enclosed is sent a Bill of Lading. The Chests have not been opened and hope they will prove agreeable and good. I enclose you the Cost of them, £692,16.4 in Case they incline to pay for them in Money, otherwise to replace them in one Year. I desire, before delivery, that you have security accordingly, either for the Paym't by Bill of Excha. Or to replace them..."*[117]

Another shipment invoiced on the same sloop with *"eight Chests cont'g 200 Firelocks with Bayonets, Slings and Cartouch boxes, and 30 b'l's Gun Powder, w'ch I wish safe to You. As y's Supply is for the two Independ't Companies, I desire You will send me a proper Receipt for them, y't I may apply to the Sec'ry of War to have them replaced, agreeable to General Braddock's Promise."*[118] The initial correspondence from Dinwiddie to William Alexander noted the shipment was the same type of arms Virginia received, unopened and unexamined. Disappointment among New York provincials was similar:

Dutch bayonet fragment, c. 1730 – 1745.
Recovered from Crown Point.
Private collection

Peter Schuyler to William Shirley
20 Septr. 1755
Sir,

I beg leave to Represent to your Excellency, that the Arms which You procured for the Regiment under my Command from the Governor of Virginia, are so extrememly bad, as to be hardly fit for service: They appear to me to be Dutch Arms, and of the worst sort, the Locks daily breaking in the common Excercise, and many of the Hammers not Steel'd: As to the Cartridge Boxes, they are almost all useless, being Slightly cover'd; They drop from the Belts in marching. I must likewise inform Your Excellency, that out of the five hundred sent from Virginia, we have lost by Desertion, and other Accidents, including the Bad not fitt for Service, one hundred and five, which will be wanted early in the Spring, and where to gett proper Arms to replace them, I know not-And am

Your Excellency's Most Obedt. Servant
Peter Schuyler

In January of 1756, Sir Charles Hardy reported to the Lords of Trade on *"Warlike Stores in the Magazine"* of Fort George in New York City. In addition to six chests belonging to the Independent companies of regulars Hardy mentions that *"what is in the possession of private People are chiefly for Indian trade."*[119] In the same year that the colony of New York acquired Dutch guns from Virginia, the city of New York imported 1,000 muskets from England which arrived by August 16th, 1755 and subsequently put into storage in City Hall.[120] These muskets would later become the subject of a bitter disagreement between General Abercromby and the city authorities. With supplies of arms at dangerously low levels, the General attempted first to impress, then purchase the city owned muskets for the 1758 campaign. After lengthy wrangling the arms were bought at an incredibly inflated price. The arms were to be purchased for no more than twenty five shillings and were sold for three pounds, five shillings, the equivalent of sixty five shillings.[121]

---

[116] Dinwiddie to the Earl of Halifax, August 7th, 1755. *Dinwiddie papers*, page 141 – 142.
[117] Dinwiddie to Alexander, May 3, 1755. *Dinwiddie papers*.
[118] Dinwiddie to Governor DeLancey, May 3, 1755. *Ibid.*
[119] *A Servant of the Crown...papers of John Appy*, page 52.
[120] *Moller, American Military Shoulder Arms*, page 233.
[121] *City of New York Muskets of 1755-1775*, by Robert E. Mulligan, page 27 – 30.

"Wilson" musket butt plate and side plate fragments, c. 1750 – 1760.
Recovered from the site of Fort Ticonderoga.
Collection of the Fort Ticonderoga Museum

Fragmentary examples of commercial military style muskets manufactured by the London based firm of Richard Wilson survive marked *"City of New York"* on the buttplate in a fashion similar to examples from New Jersey. An orderly book entry for New York provincials in Van Schaick's company of Delancey's Regiment dated October 14, 1758 stipulates that *"All the arms marked New York to be kept in the Regiment & Kings arms taken from the men & be delivered in the store in their room."*[122]

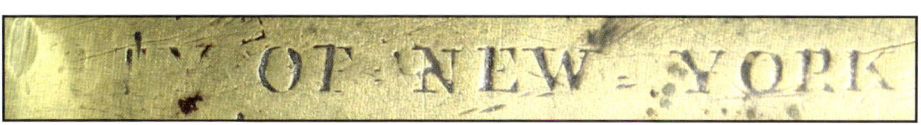

A "City of New York" marked butt plate from a Wilson musket.
Courtesy of the American Revolution Center, Benninghoff Collection

Using the proceeds from the musket sale in June of 1758 the city's Common Council bought *"five hundred of the subscription arms Lately Imported in this City"*, and then sent off to England for an additional *"four hundred and fifty Small arms"* as well as fire engines and buckets.[123] On December 18, 1758 the city's Common Council ordered Nicolas Roosevelt to be paid for *"marking of five hundred and fifty Small arms."*[124] At least 550 of the replacement arms marked by Roosevelt in 1758 appear to have also been produced by Wilson of London. Unlike the original 1,000 stands which were likely engraved *"City of New York"* in London, these arms were marked locally with Arabic numerals on both bayonets and buttplates. An inventory of these arms dating from 1775 show numbers from 451 to 1,000 with an additional notation penciled on the back cover that reads *"William Livingston at Eliz[abeth]town has a musket No. 450 the maker Wilson London. Que[ry] is not this one of the City Arms."*[125] Although it is unlikely that the group of arms marked by Roosevelt saw any service during the French and Indian war, a New York City-owned musket marked *"796"* survives in the United States Military Academy collection at West Point. Records indicate that this musket was removed from City Hall and placed with a Mr. Duychinck in April of 1775, who later returned the musket for Continental Army service. With its "N-Y" over "J. REG" brand in the stock, this musket was likely one of the 434 muskets issued to the 1st New York Regiment for service in the American Revolution.[126] New York's provincials continued to be at least partially armed out of Royal Stores for the 1759 campaign. A warrant signed by Jeffrey Amherst instructed Ordnance Comptroller Furnis to issue *"Arms for Two Thousand & Sixty Men"* to *"John Johnston Esq. Colonel of the New York Troops"* on 18th May, 1759.[127]

In addition to the Wilson muskets purchased for the city of New York, a wide variety of arms were available on the commercial market. A total of 2,250 firearms were purchased by the colony for the 1758 campaign.[128] Contemporary newspaper advertisements show that *"Muskets with Bayonets, and Buckaneers"* as well as *"neat fuzees & common fowling pieces"* were available in the colony.[129]

---

[122] *Muskets in the American Revolution*, page 141. Original manuscript in Fort Ticonderoga Museum Collections FT 1997.027.

[123] Moller, *American Military Shoulder Arms*, page 234.

[124] *Ibid.*

[125] *New York Historical Society Quarterly Bulletin*, Vol. XXIII, No. 1. January, 1939.

[126] Moller, *American Military Shoulder Arms*, page 234.

[127] *W.O.* 34/70, page 55.

[128] DeLancey to Pitt, 1 June, 1758. *Pitt, I*, page 264, as quoted by *Cardwell*, page 261.

[129] *New York Mercury*, May 8, 1758.

North Carolina

The North Carolina provincials, who first arrived to assist Virginia's small army in 1754, were only partially armed and received muskets from both Virginia and Maryland stores:

"WILLIAMSBURG, June 20. This Morning one hundred Stand of Arms, with Ammunition,&c. were sent from this Place for Hampton, there to be shipped for Alexandria, for the Use of the North Carolina Forces."[130]

"There were 150 Muskets sent hence to the Carolina Troops the Summer before last...Col. Innes, as appears by the Armourer's Account, has returned only 132, but 28 of them have Bayonets, and are much better than what he borrowed. 4th March 1756 Hor.o Sharpe."[131]

North Carolina's Governor Arthur Dobbs also appealed to the British government for military supplies and small arms, since *"there is a Number of Small Arms in the Tower of London that are not of an Assortment proper for His Majesty's Forces here, he therefore humbly prays that His Majesty will be pleased to grant One Thousand of those Spare Small Arms, with their Bayonets, Swords and other Accoutrements to enable the Colony to give useful Arms to the Troops raised for the present Expedition..."*[132] Dobbs' request was granted, and the next day, the following was recorded:

By the Lieutenant General, Surveyor General, Clerk of Ordnance.

"The Surveyor General having pursuant to Reference of the 25th considered his Majesty's Order in Council of the 21st Instant Reported that there are in Store at the Tower a number of Dutch Musquets with Bayonets bought in Holland in 1741 which are of a pattern quite different from those now Issued to his Majesty's Forces here, that he was therefore of Opinion there can be no objection to their being Issued upon receiving His Majesty's Warrant for so doing and to authorize the Board to receive the Value therof from Arthur Dobbs Esqr. Or to insert the charge in the next Estimate to Parliament. That the Value of the Musquets and Bayonets may be esteemed at 16.6 each but that there will be a further charge for Chests Package &ca. That as to the Swords prayed for by the Memorialist, they are not within the Department of this office to furnish, that if the Memorialist means by other accoutrements Slings and Cartouch Boxes, there are sufficient of

---

[130] July 18, 1754 The Pennsylvania Gazette.

[131] *Maryland Assembly Proceedings*, page 318. Feb. 23 – May 22, 1756.

[132] W.O. 55/354, 21st June, 1754. *At the Court at Kensington*, page 302.

Ordnance "Figure of Eight" cutlass for Sea Service, c. 1750 – 1760.
Private collection

Tann'd Slings in Store that can be Issued That the Cartouch Boxes in Store are all of one Pattern tho they differ in Size and Price according to the Number of Holes they contain therefore if they are to be Issued he recommended those of 12 Holes. Ordered that a Representation be made hereon to His Majesty in Council and that an Estimate of the Charge of such particulars as can be furnished out of the Stores in the Tower be inserted therein amounting to £1016 13. 4 22 June 1754."[133]

An additional two thousand stands of arms were added to the shipment for the Colony of Virginia, but a problem arose since the Tower had *"no Swords for Land Service this being a Species of Store never furnished by this Office."* Infantry swords were generally purchased on the regimental level *"but if on this Emergency Sea Service Swords will do which are a sort of half Basket Iron Hilt Black'd, the stores can furnish enough."*[134] This most likely describes what is known as the "Figure Eight" configuration that dominated naval cutlasses in British service of the period. The final details were sorted out that same evening, and *"Sat: Night June 29th 1754"* a warrant was issued for *"3000 Musquets and Bayonets of Dutch Fabrick, 3000 Tanned Leather Slings for the same, 3000 Cartouch Boxes with Belts and Frogs, 3000 Sea Service Swords with Tanned Leather belts together with 120 Halberts and 80 Drums to be delivered to Arthur Dobbs esqr. Governor of our Province of North Carolina."*[135] These arms arrived in the colony by December of 1754 as shown by the records of the North Carolina Assembly on December 16, 1754[136] *"Mr. Starkey produced to this House an Accompt from Capt Thomas Pearson for the Freight of One Thousand Arms Swords &c, from his Majesty for the use of the Province."* These muskets were then distributed to North Carolina's newly-formed provincials who went to Virginia to assist Braddock.

Ammunition still seems to have been in short supply for the Carolinians as a letter dated May 5, 1755, from Virginia's Lt. Governor Dinwiddie to North Carolina's Governor Dobbs indicates that the North Carolina's provincial troops in Virginia could be *"supplied…with powder and Shott…"* from Virginia stores. This shortage of ammunition seems to have continued for quite some time according to a letter from Governor Dobbs to the Board of Trade dated December 15, 1755:

"the 1000 arms I got when I came over will be distributed to the five companies raised and to be raised and to the Militia of the exposed Counties and near the sea coast for our Defense ammunition or lead we have none but from hand to mouth and very little in the Merchants hands…"[137]

Not only was powder and shot hard to come by, but the original musket shipment was quickly disappearing.

"When I came over His Majesty was pleased to give 1000. stand of arms and accoutrements for the use of the Province you will see by the return of the militia that they are not half armed and those they have very bad. The Companies we raised here together with the arms which were carried off by Deserters have taken of these near 400. and I sent 150 to the western Frontier to arm the militia of two Counties there, and another frontier County will want half as much, and I have sent & ordered to be sent near 100. more to the Batteries and Militia at Cape Fear, and the remainder will be wanted to distribute to the Militia along the Sea Coast, so that it would be necessary to have a supply of 2000. arms at least to supply the militia, many would be willing to pay for them, as they wou'd expect to get good

---

[133] *W.O.* 47/43, page 373.
[134] *W.O.* 55/354, page 304.
[135] *Ibid.*, page 305.
[136] *Colonial Records*, page 237.
[137] *Colonial Records of North Carolina*, pages 461 – 462.

Halberd head and ground iron, c. 1750 – 1770.
Private collection

arms at a reasonable price from the Crown- and we ought to have an immediate supply of 20. barrils of Gunpowder at least to be able to make a proper defense if attacked, as you will see by the return of the powder duty..."

Dobbs to the Earl of Loudon July 10, 1756.[138]

By the time the 1758 campaign started, the British planned another major thrust towards the French Fort Duquesne, this time under General John Forbes, Colonel of the 17th Regiment. The North Carolina provincials sent north for the Forbes expedition arrived at least partially unarmed. General Forbes wrote that *"I have ordered the North Carolina troops to march to Fort Loudon to receive arms tents &c."*[139] In a letter to Washington dated July 30, 1758; Charles Smith reported that at Fort Loudon (Fort Loudon, Virginia, not to be confused with forts of the same name in Tennessee and Pennsylvania) *"Thare is 25 of the Caralinians here & has not one Gun among them..."*[140]

As Forbes and his force of regulars and provincials methodically worked their way closer to Duquesne, the French removed most of their stores, and razing the majority of their fortifications, abandoned their position. On November 25, 1758, British troops took possession of the Forks of the Ohio and soon began erecting new fortifications. Following this campaign, the lack of arms in North Carolina continued to worsen as *"The Companies that served upon the Ohio last year having been disbanded by Act of Assembly Upon their return into this Province and a Gratuity of £5 having been allowed to all such as should return into the province and as the most part of them upon their return through Virginia dispersed and carried off their Arms, and a very small number returned to receive that Gratuity-"*

Arthur Dobbs to the Speaker and the Gentlemen of the Assembly 17 May 1759"[141]

As the Cherokee war heated up the Carolina back country, North Carolina again found its provincials short of the necessary small arms: *"Some of our (North Carolina) provincials are in this neighborhood, but their cloathing is not come up, and they are in want of arms. When they are to march is uncertain."*[142] This hampered deployment for quite a while, and by September 17, 1761 the Pennsylvania Gazette reported that *"Colonel Waddle was marched for fort Dobbs, with such part of his regiment as was provided with arms..."*

---

[138] *W.O.* 47/43, page 373.

[139] *Writings of General John Forbes*, page 147.

[140] Charles Smith to Washington, July 30, 1758. *George Washington papers.*

[141] *Colonial Records of North Carolina.*

[142] Salisbury, NC. July 26, 1761. *New York Mercury.*

Pennsylvania

Following Braddock's failed expedition against Fort Duquesne in the summer of 1755, fierce Indian and French raids multiplied in the Pennsylvania and Virginia back country. Newly-arrived Anglican minister Thomas Barton wrote that *"Not a Man in Ten is able to purchase a Gun…Not a House in Twenty has a Door with either Lock or Bolt to it."*[143] William Allen summed up the situation when he wrote to London merchants David Barclay and Sons:

P*hilad. 21st July 1755*

Gentlemen,

The late Defeat of the King's Forces has put every thing in the greatest confusion in this province, to the great Scandal of the English Name - General Braddock with an advanced part of his Army was attacked by one third of his Number of Indians & French & put to the Rout; one half of his party either killed or wounded… Could our Assembly be prevailed onto raise the money, not less than 3000 men would have gone out of this Province, who as they fight for their Country, and are more used to the Woods & have a better notion of the Indian method of Fighting, would behave in another manner than the English Troops have done… As there is some appearance of our being roused from our Lethargy, we are about putting the province in some small posture of Defence- But as we are much in want of arms, we are desire to send for a Thousand musquets, which we are told may be bought at the Tower from 11/ to 13/ a piece with Bayonets & Cartouch boxes, being such as the Army have formerly used- We are informed that the East India Compa. purchases such for their Settlements- We beg there fore that you would purchase the above Quantity on the best Terms you can & Ship them by the very first opportunity this Fall if possible, taking care they are well inspected that they are good & fit for Service…"[144]

In a document entitled *"List of Applications for Stores & CA Defending Before the Committee. May 1756"* the state of affairs in *"Pensilvania"* were described as quite dire: *"The Govr represents that this Province is in no Condition to defend itself, but must fall an easy Prey to almost any Invader, without the British Parliament interposes and by proper Laws establishes Order & Discipline amongst the People."*[145]

Munitions began to flow into Pennsylvania. Although there is no evidence of the purchase of arms from the Tower by Barclay and Sons, that firm did procure a large quantity of ordnance for the Colony the next year. Benjamin Franklin wrote to James Read on November 2, 1755 that *"I receiv'd your Letter per Mr. Tea, and one just now per Express. I am glad to hear the Arms are well got up: They are the best that we could procure, I wish they were better. But they are well fortified, will bear a good Charge, and I should imagine they may do good Service with Swan or Buck Shot, if not so fit for single Ball…I have however done what I could in sending about to purchase Arms, &c. for the Supply of the Frontiers, and can now spare you 50 more, which shall send up to-morrow, with some Flints, Lead Swan shot, and a Barrell of Gunpowder…The 50 Arms now sent are all furnish'd with Staples for Sling Straps, that if the Governor should order a Troop or Company of Rangers on Horseback, the Piece may be slung at the Horseman's Back."*[146] Pennsylvania acquired firearms from a dizzying array of sources in 1756 (seventeen total), in quantities as small as two from Leonard Melchoir, to the year's largest purchase of 1,500 Fire Arms and fifteen *"18 Lbrs"* cannon from Barclay & Sons.[147] Along with the 4,789 total firearms received that year were 29 cannon, 14 swivels, 710 tomahawks, 66 Pistols, 13 wall guns, 68 cutlasses, and ammunition. A letter from the provincial Commissioners to Robert Hunter Morris indicates that *"7 Swivel Blunderbusses"* were being sent for the use of *"the Battoes."*[148]

---

[143] Thomas Barton to Richard Peters, Huntington, July 30, 1755. *Richard Peters papers*, IV, 36. Historical Society of Pennsylvania MS Collection.

[144] *William Allen Letterbook, Shippen Family Papers*, #595C. Historical Society of Pennsylvania MS Collection.

[145] *Military Affairs in North America*, page 168 – 169.

[146] *Papers of Benjamin Franklin*, Volume 6: Nov. 2, 1755.

[147] An Account of Arms and Ammunition 1756: *Pennsylvania Archives*, 1756, page 25.

[148] *Papers of Benjamin Franklin*, Volume 6: May 15, 1756.

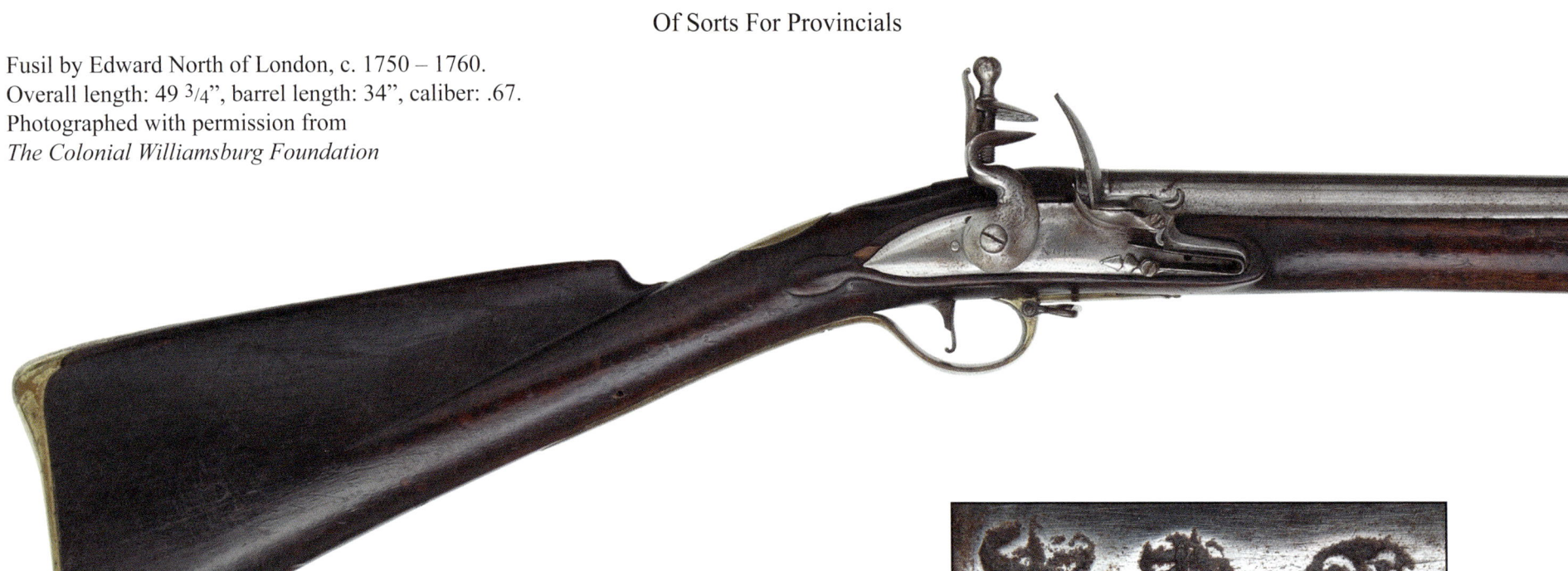

Fusil by Edward North of London, c. 1750 – 1760.
Overall length: 49 3/4", barrel length: 34", caliber: .67.
Photographed with permission from
The Colonial Williamsburg Foundation

The mark of Thomas Hawley (II) of London.

Munitions also came from Royal Stores:

MEMORANDUM.
The Governor, on the twenty-eight of April, wrote a Letter to General Shirley to request One Thousand Arms, having heard that Ten Thousand were arrived at Boston for the Defence of the Colonies ; this he did at the Instance of the Commissioners, and the
Letter was sent by Express, and is as follows:
PHILADELPHIA, 28th April, 1756.

Sir: As the Province is in the utmost Distress for want of Arms, the few we have being miserably bad, and those ordered from England not arrived, the Commissioners for laying out the Sixty Thousand Pounds have desired mo to represent this to your Excellency by express, and having received Information of the Arrival of a large Quantity of Arms at Boston, to request of you that they may in their Great Exigency be favored with a thousand, or something less if so many cannot be spared, and that you would be pleased to give your Orders for that Purpose to those whc the Charge of them. No Province, I assure your Excellency want a Supply of Arms so much as this, apprehensive as we an attack from the Ohio every Day, and as I hope these Art graciously sent by his Majesty for the Defence of the Colony can rely on your Excellency's Goodness to extend this Favour to issue your Orders by the bearer, who will go with all Dispatch to Boston with them, and pay the Charges of Shipping...

I am, Sir, Your Excellency's most Obedient humble Sen [Servant]
ROBT. H. MORRIS [149]

---

[149] *Minutes of the Provincial Council of Pennsylvania*, Volume VII, page 109 – 110.

American Weapons of the French and Indian War

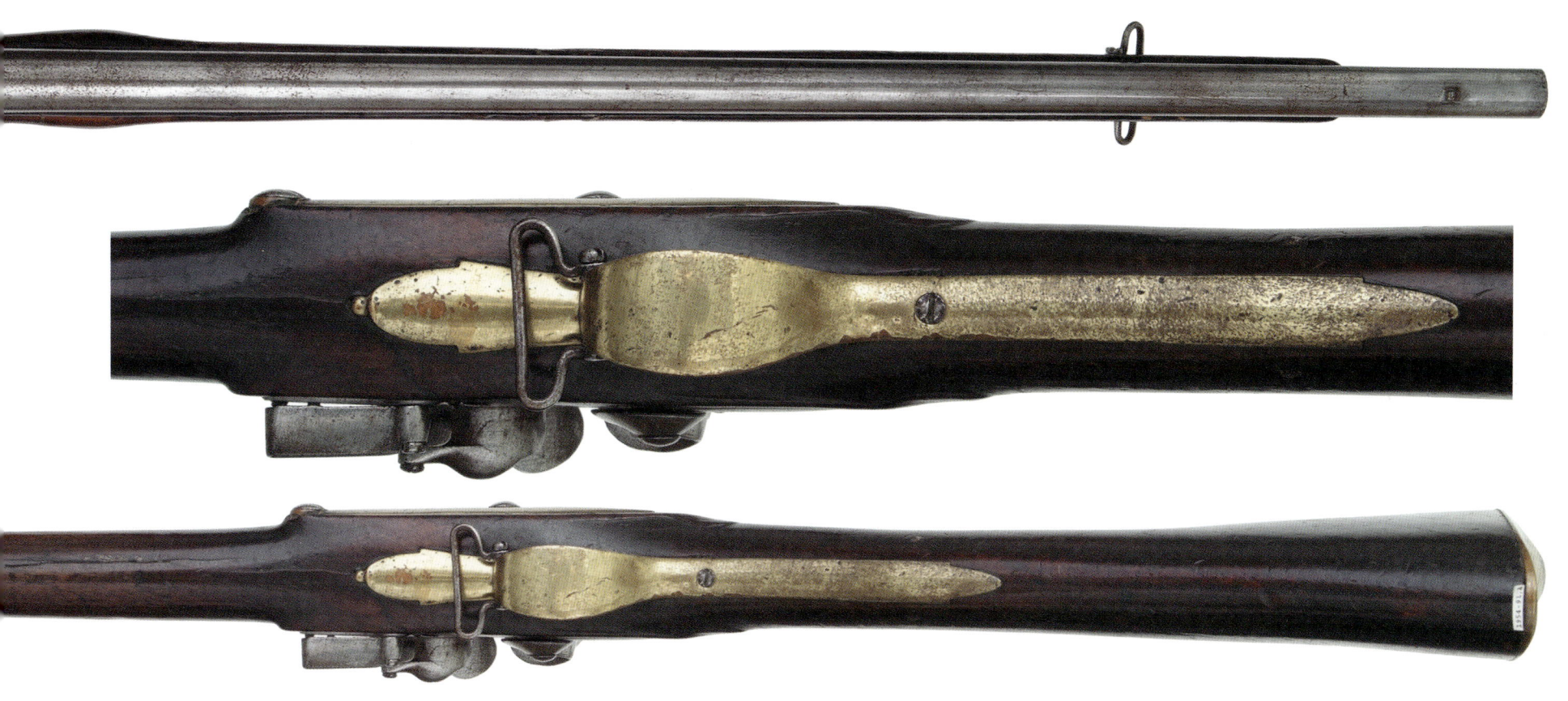

A letter from General Shirley to Governor Morris arrived, informing that 600, (not the 1,000 stands of arms that had been requested) were to be delivered to Pennsylvania store keepers:

New York, May 2nd, 1756.

"I am favoured with your Letter of the 20th of April, and have thereupon sent orders to the comptroller of his Majesty's Ordinance at Boston, to deliver 600 stands of arms, with a propper Proportion of Ammunition to any Person who shall be authorized by your Honour's Government to Receive and indent for the same on behalf of the Province, according to the Tenour of the inclosed Form of indent."[150]

Inventories confirm that the six hundred *"King's Arms"..."From Boston"* were received that year.[151] These King's Arms were Pennsylvania's share of the 10,000 *"Land Service Muskets of the King's Pattern with Brass Furniture, Double Bridle Locks Wood Rammers with Bayonets & Scabbards and Tann'd Leather Slings...Cartouch Boxes with Straps of 12 Holes..."*[152] distributed by William Shirley that year.

---

[150] *Minutes of the Provincial Council of Pennsylvania*, Volume VII, page 111.

[151] An Account of Arms and Ammunition 1756. *Pennsylvania Archives 1756*, page 25.

[152] *W.O.* 55/412, page 3. Nov. 12, 1755.

Aside from the regulation muskets, contemporary documents reinforce the notion of a variety of arms being in service at this time, including *"Fuses or light arms"*:

You are also to send out, from time to time, one or more Companies, as you shall judge proper, to range and Scour the woods Westward, as far as they can be accomodated with Provisions in proper Quantities and Qualitys; which Parties are to be made up of Detachments from such garrisons as you shall think fit, but not to consist of less than fifty in Each party, and to be Commanded by such of the officers as you shall appoint, and you are to furnish them with proper Orders ant Instructions to search for and annoy the Enemy Indians, and to recover as many Prisoners as they can, and to be Particularly Careful in their marches not to be Surprised. You will receive from the Commissioners one Hundred muskets, with their Accoutrements, and two Hundred Fuzees or light Arms, with theirs. The former are to be Distributed among the Garrisons there they are most wanted, taking the Officers' receipts, and you we to send down all the Arms that are bad and Defective. The Fuzees are Intended for the ranging Service, and You are to be Accountable for the whole. A Quantity of Amunition & provision will also be sent up, and the Commissioners are to follow and observe our Orders and Directions in the Destribution thereof.

By his Honour's Command,
ROBT-H. MORRIS. W- PETERS, Milli- Secretary.
PMM 4th June, 1756."[153]

Newspaper accounts confirm this mixture of types:

"...By Lieutenant Colonel Armstrong Returns, it appears that there was on the 11th of last Month 57 effective Arms, 50 Pound of Powder, and 100 Weight of Lead, in Fort Granville. Three Hundred Weight of Powder, and 700 Weight of Lead, were sent up by the Commissioners to Carlisle on the 24th of June, to be distributed by Col. Armstrong, among the Forts on the West Side of Sasquehanna, as he should judge necessary, and we are informed that he had accordingly supply them all with an additional Quantity, before the taking of Fort Granville. At the same time 100 of the new Muskets, and 200 of the Fuses, imported from England for the Use of the Province Forces, were likewise sent up to supply such Arms as were defective."[154]

A document titled *"A return of Artillery, Small Arms & Sundry Stores belonging to the Province..."* dated *"May ye 4th, 1758"* indicates that Pennsylvania owned *"Musquets"* remaining in stores that were equipped with *"Bayonets...Slings... Cartrage Boxes...Worms"* and fired one ounce balls as well as *"Fuzes"* equipped with *"Care boxes...Slings...Worms"* that fired 3/4 ounce balls.[155] Although equipped with slings and boxes, the *"Fuzes"* included in this list do not appear to have been fitted with bayonets as they are not mentioned in the return.

Three years after Braddock's death, Pennsylvania found itself the base of operations for the second major British attempt against Fort Duquesne under General John Forbes in 1758. British Quartermaster St. Clair advised George Stevenson of York County that when recruiting for the provincial Service *"the Men to furnish their own Arms, for wch., if good, they will have a proper allowance."*[156]

---

[153] *Minutes of the Provincial Council of Pennsylvania*, Volume VII, page 161.
[154] *Pennsylvania Gazette*, August 19, 1756.
[155] Historical Society of Pennsylvania. Frank B. Nead Collection, # 447.
[156] *Forbes Papers.* St. Clair to George Stevenson, May 5, 1758. Box #3.

American Weapons of the French and Indian War

Contemporary newspapers give descriptions of what some civilian-owned firearms looked like. An ad describes a *"Borrowed or stolen"* Lancaster County gun belonging to one John Harris in the Pennsylvania Gazette, dated October 25, 1759 *"a certain Gun, stocked with wild red Cherry Tree, about four Feet long in the Barrel, near one Foot next the Breech square [octagonal], and the other Parts of the Barrel filed round, and near the said square Part the Gun is brazed, and the Brass appears on the Barrel, and on the Side Plate marked thus I H with an Iron Sight behind after the Rifle Form, and a raised Silver Sight before, pretty long, and neatly finished off, as is the whole gun."*

Military style firearms were also available in Pennsylvania. None other than Benjamin Franklin advertised on March 8, 1748 in the Pennsylvania Gazette that he had *"A Parcel of good Muskets, all well fitted with Bayonets, Belts and Cartouch Boxes, and Buff Slings to cast over the Shoulder, very useful to such as have Occasion to ride with their Arms"* for sale. Acknowledging the absence of shipments from England for the ensuing campaign; General Forbes warned Pennsylvania's Governor Denny that the colony's recruits would have to be equipped with arms that were *"the best that can be found in the Province"*.[157] Forbes requisitioned *"Two Hundred and Eighteen Light Fuzees"* from Pennsylvania stores for his hoped for allied Indians and noted that *"There will remain in your Store more Arms than will Compleat the Forces proposed to be raised by this Province, besides 2,000 Arms, which I have an Account of being embarked for the Service of this Expedition."*[158]

These demands, coupled with Prime Minister Pitt's 1758 proclamation which gave the Colonies freedom from arming their own troops, caused great friction between the Pennsylvania legislature and Forbes. Despite this, Pennsylvania mustered three battalions of provincials, some of whom seem to have received arms that were quite poor. A return for John McClughan's company in Lancaster, dated June 4, 1758 indicates that no cartouch boxes, belts, slings, tomahawks, tents or knapsacks were present. The 93 guns are described as *"never prov-* [proofed] *and Deemed bad."*[159] The preoccupation with proof testing of the Province's arms may have stemmed from previous bad experiences with low quality arms that exploded upon firing. Pennsylvania Commisary Young's Journal noted three *"burst"* muskets in stores at Fort Norris in July of 1756.[160]

Another return for Captain Benjamin Noxon's Company lists 66 *"Guns Rec."* [received] and 30 *"wanting"* to complete the enlisted men and non-commissioned officers, again *"deemed bad."* As with McClughan's return, the quantities listed for cartouch boxes, belts, and gun slings are *"none."* At the bottom of the return Lieutenant Colonel John Armstrong of the Pennsylvania provincials notes *"I have examined the Arms the Captain's Noxon & McClughan's Companies are possess'd off, and find them Heavy and unwieldy for the present Service tho with some necessary repairs may be used, being capable of receiv.g [receiving] with a Bullet some Slugs or Buckshott"* which likely indicates the usage of full-sized smooth bore arms."*[161]

The 1758 Journal of James Burd mentions *"poudder horns, pouches"* and cartridge boxes were being used by Pennsylvania's provincials, as well as reinforcing that some of the detachments had *"no province arms fit for use."*[162] Unlike most other colonies, Pennsylvanians seem have been partially equipped with rifles. Colonel Armstrong noted the allied Indians were desirous of rifles and that *"the Indian Capt was gratified and got a rifle from one of the soldiers."*[163]

In a letter from Carlyle dated June 3, 1758, Colonel Henry Bouquet recommended that *"until arms should arrive from England, I think it advisable to persuade every Man that has a Good Gun, or Rifle to bring it with him."* A group from the First Pennsylvania Battalion, including one Jonathan Hill and another provincial soldier named John Miller were advertised as deserters on June 15, 1758, in the Pennsylvania Gazette. Their party *"all had their Regimentals, green faced with red, and Hill and Miller had new Rifles."* This mixture of firearms requiring varying sizes of ammunition must have caused logistical problems, as a letter from Bouquet to Forbes notes that *"A large part of the provincials are armed with grooved rifles and have their molds. Lead in bars will suit them better than bullets."*[164]

Ball mold, date unknown.
Robert Nittolo collection

---

[157] Forbes to Denny, March 20, 1758. *Writings of Forbes*. page 58.

[158] Forbes to Denny, April 20, 1758. *Ibid.*, page 66 – 67.

[159] Return Capn. McClughans Compy, Lancaster, 4th June, 1758. *Forbes papers*. Box #4.

[160] *Commissy Young's Journal from Reading, to Sundry Forts in Berks & Northrn Counties from Pennsylvania Archives*, Series 1, Volume 2, page 675 – 681.

[161] Return Captain Noxons Company, Lancaster. June 4, 1758. *Forbes papers*, Box #4.

[162] *Burds Journal*. 10 March, 1758. from *Pennsylvania Archives*, Series 1, volume 3, p 352 – 357.

[163] Colonel John Armstrong to the Executive Council. Carlyle, 5 May, 1757. *Minutes of the Provincial Council From the Organization to the Termination of the Proprietary Government*, volume 7, page 505.

[164] *British Military Flintlock Rifles*, page 15 – 16.

"Kittanning Destroyed" Medal (restrike), c. 1800 – 1820.
The Kittanning destroyed medal commemorates the 1756 raid on Kittanning by Pennsylvania's forces under Colonel John Armstrong.
The Colonial Williamsburg Foundation. Gift of Ruth P. and Joseph R. Lasser.

A mixture of smooth bore arms and rifles among Pennsylvania provincials is further corroborated by a description of target practice exercise by an officer of the 60th Regiment from March of 1759: *"All the Penss that fire have not Riffles, nor do those that have make the best Shots…"*[165] At least one of the bullets recovered from Fort Ligonier in Pennsylvania had been fired from a rifled gun which featured *"eight lands and groove marks. It measured 0.56 inch."*[166] Other shot recovered from Fort Ligonier included a total of 52 sizes, with large quantities of buck or swan shot (.32-39"), carbine (.62" for a .65-.70" bore) and musket (.69" for a .75-80" bore).[167]

General Forbes *"was obliged to purchase a great many Arms, Tents & c, for the Provinicalls"*[168] due to an inadequate supply of arms from England that arrived late. Numerous receipts for privately-purchased arms survive in Forbes' papers, however the vast majority of them are generically termed *"fusees"*, *"muskets"* or *"guns"* although the receipt for *"31 Fuzees with Bayonets…Bot. Of McJanett and McMurtie…"* by *"Mr. William West By Order of His Excellency General Forbes"* may have been intended for provincial use given the inclusion of bayonets.[169] When arms finally did arrive from the Tower for Forbes, they were vaguely described as: *"Musquets with Wood Rammers - Bayonets and Tann'd Leather slings"* in a warrant signed by William Pitt dated January 5th, 1758.[170] Further inventories in Forbes' papers fail to identify the specific type of arms he received, however the cartouch boxes are listed as having *"18 Holes."*[171] General Forbes must have heaved a sigh of relief when he announced in June of 1758 the long awaited *"Store Ship with Arms, Tents, Ammunition, & Artillery & ca. Arrived here the 11th, which enables me to sett out directly for the frontiers…"*[172]

Despite his wide-ranging purchases in Philadelphia and the additional arms from Maryland, Forbes notified Bouquet that he proposed to *"send of to morrow 1000 Stand of our new arms, and 200 more tents, which I hope will be more than wee will have occasion for in that way."*[173]

---

[165] *British Military Flintlock Rifles*, page 16.
[166] *Archaeological Investigation of Fort Ligonier*, page 109.
[167] *Ibid.*, page 109.
[168] Forbes to Pitt. *Writings of General John Forbes*, page 118.
[169] *Forbes Papers*, Box #3, No. 9. Mc.Jannet & Co., May 8, 1758.
[170] *W.O.* 55/412. page 191.
[171] *Forbes Papers*, "A Proportion of Ordnance and Stores for Pensilvania", June 13, 1758. Box #4.
[172] Forbes to Pitt, June 17th, 1759. *Writings of John Forbes*, page 116 – 117.
[173] Forbes to Bouquet. June 16th, 1759. *Writings of John Forbes*, page 115.

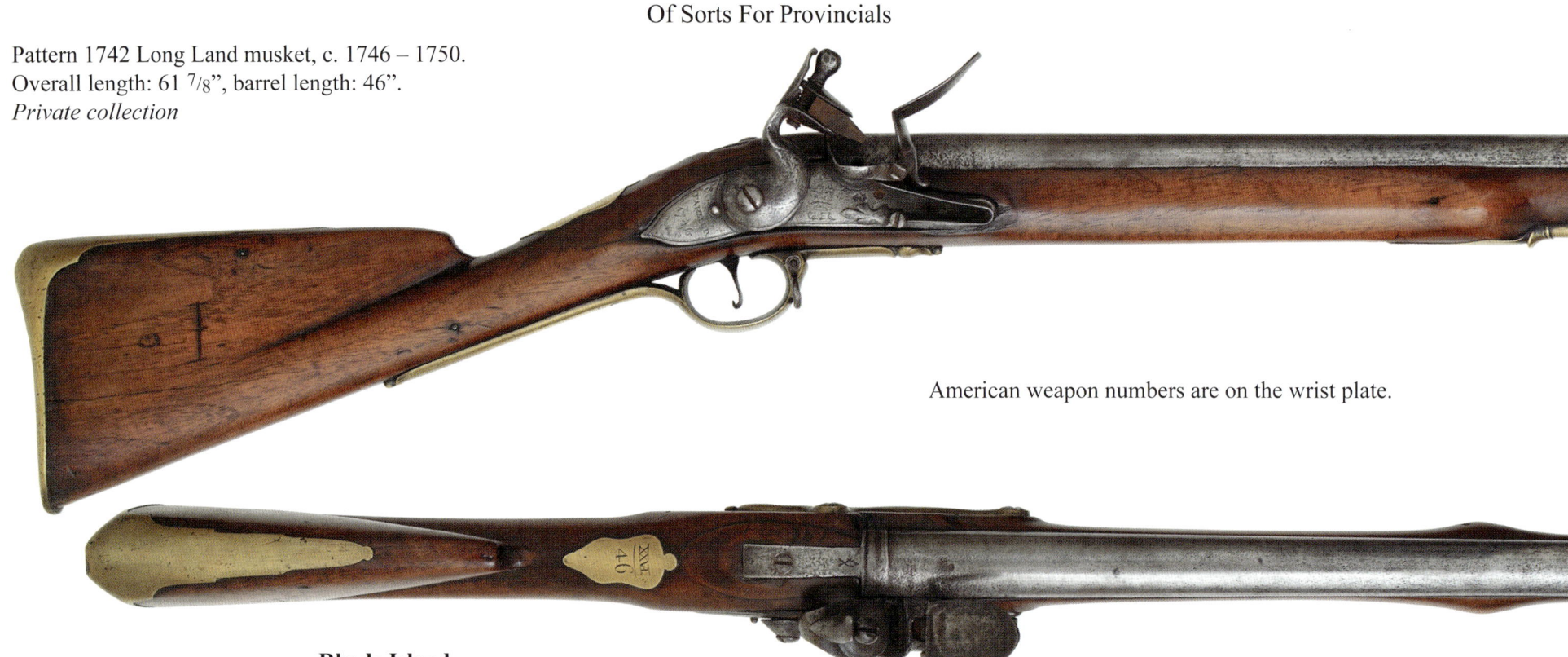

Pattern 1742 Long Land musket, c. 1746 – 1750.
Overall length: 61 7/8", barrel length: 46".
Private collection

American weapon numbers are on the wrist plate.

Rhode Island

Although tiny in size, Rhode Island mustered provincials throughout the French and Indian War. A report dated May 12, 1756 lists *"28 Pistols, 17 Small Arms… 9 Cartridge Boxes…9 Powder Horns, 18 Cartouch Boxes…4 Cutlasses"* among other stores in the colony.[174] The need for a supply of munitions was apparent, and Rhode Island requested *"such a Quantity of Small Arms and Powder as to His Majesty shall seem meet"* from the Royal government that same month.[175] Ordnance Comptroller James Furnis' letter book confirms that the colony received *"small arms & ca. delivered to them out of His Majesty's Stores."*[176] This is further corroborated by an extract of a letter dated March 3, 1757[177] which mentions *"Arms delivered for the Governments of the Massachusetts Bay, Rhode Island and New Hampshire."* The arms referenced must be a portion of the 10,000 stands of *"Land Service Muskets of the King's Pattern with Brass Furniture, Double Bridle Locks Wood Rammers with Bayonets & Scabbards and Tann'd Leather Slings…Cartouch Boxes with Straps of 12 Holes…"* received in 1756.

Commercial purchases supplemented armaments from the government. A document entitled *"An account of Sundry Necessary Small Stores, Small Arms, Tents and other Camp Equipage Furnished by the Colony of Rhode Island to the Troops by them raised for His Majesty's Service in the Years 1757 and 1758. For which the said Colony Humbly Prays to be reimbursed"* lists the most expensive single expenditure of 1757 as *"…220 Small Arms Purchased @ £ 35-10…7810"* although this price was eclipsed by the cost of 1,000 blankets totaling *"£ 13500"* in 1758.[179] Rhode Island's provincials continued to be at least partially armed out of Royal Stores for the duration of the war. A warrant signed by Jeffrey Amherst instructed Ordnance Comptroller Furnis to issue *"One Hundred Eighty Seven Muskets"* to *"Colonel Babcock of the Rhode Island Regiment"* on 24 May, 1759.[180]

---

[174] Report May 12, 1756. *Rhode Island Historical Society MS Colonial Militia Collection*, MSS 673 SG1.

[175] List of Applications for Stores & CA Defending Before the Committee. May 1756; *Military Affairs in North America*, page 168 – 169.

[176] Furnis Letter book, February 9th, 1757. page 70.

[177] *W.O.* 47/49. page 278.

[178] *W.O.* 55/412, page 3. Nov. 12, 1755.

[179] *Rhode Island Historical Society Richard Partridge Collection*, MSS 9001-P.

[180] *W.O.* 34/70, page 58.

The mark of Edward Jordan of Birmingham.

The iron rammer, nose band and front rammer pipe are working life additions.

American Weapons of the French and Indian War

Of Sorts For Provincials

Iron mounted Dutch musket, c. 1710 – 1730.
Possibly restocked c. 1730 – 1740.
Overall length: 60", barrel length: 44 1/2", caliber: .80.
Robert Nittolo collection

Stag handled hanger, c. 1690 – 1720.
Jim Mullins collection

South Carolina

Prior to the French and Indian War South Carolina and especially her capital, Charles-Towne boasted a comparatively strong and well-organized militia tradition, in part due to the white population's fear of slave rebellion and the perceived risk to the Colony's Capitol posed by foreign navies. By the beginning of the war, Charles-Towne itself had not only a powder magazine, fortifications, but also a troop of horse, an Artillery company and a store of public arms. At least two extant specimens of *"So. Carolina"* marked muskets survive. Both are Dutch in manufacture, and feature different locks and mountings. Possibly they are from the shipment listed below:

"An Account of the Ordnance & Stores sent to the Province of South Carolina in the year 1731 by the Ship Loyal Judith Robert Simpson Master, Persuant to His Majestys Orders in Council bearing date 14th December..."[181] lists:

Dutch Musquets with Bayonets ...300
Cartouch Boxes 300
Swords 300

Despite being marked in a similar fashion, one of the surviving *"So. Carolina"* marked muskets stylistically predates the other. An earlier, rounded lock and top-mounted bayonet lug, as well as iron mounts would seem to indicate that this gun predates the Dutch muskets purchased in 1741. Ordnance records show the Dutch arms purchased by Britain in 1741 were exclusively brass-mounted with flat locks. In addition, the brass-mounted, flat-locked specimen has several cosmetic similarities to iron-mounted Dutch arms imported for the Irish Ordinance in 1715.[182] Fragments of a particular variety of English stag handled hanger frequently show up in South Carolina, indicating widespread use during the eighteenth century. A nearly identical fragment is on view in the Charleston museum. These swords, possibly included on the inventory at left, feature a relatively short blade, and decorative figures cast into the brass guard. There is no substantial evidence of swords being issued to South Carolina provincials during the French and Indian war and these artifacts likely date to usage in years prior to that conflict.

---

[181] *C.O. 5/657.*
[182] *Dutch Muskets for Ireland, 1706 – 1715.* by Howard L. Blackmore, page 80.

American Weapons of the French and Indian War

Excavated guard fragment.
Private collection

Further evidence of arms shipments to South Carolina includes *"An Account of Ordnance & Stores sent to the Province of South Carolina in the year 1739 by the ship Prince Galley John Bowles Master, Pursuant to His Majestys Order in Council bearing date 31st July 1738"*[183] which lists:

Land Service Musquets of Sorts with Brass Furniture and Bayonets............ 1000
Cartouch Boxes.. 1000

Given the description as being *"of Sorts"* instead of being invoiced as *"of the King's Pattern"* it can be deduced that these arms were not regulation Land Service muskets. A later shipment dated September 28, 1739 was *"sent to General Oglethorpe by the Ship Charming Philley for the Defence and Security of the Province of South Caronlina and Colony of Georgia"* included 1,000 *"Musquets with Bayonets of the Kings pattern with brass furniture."*[184]

Non-Ordnance arms were also procured. In January 1744, an order for 500 muskets and bayonets for the militia was placed and the Assembly requested *"his Excellency to give Directions that Mr Richard Wilson of London, Gunmaker, may be employed to send the same hither."*[185]

As war loomed on the horizon for Britain's colonies, the South Carolina legislature ordered a report of the *"Committee appointed to inspect the Condition of the Public Arms"*:

---

[183] *C.O.* 5/657.

[184] *Ibid.*, page 66.

[185] *The Wilsons: Gunmakers to Empire 1730 – 1832.* by DeWitt Bailey II, page 85/15.

February 8th 1754

Report, That your Committee have pursuant to the order of the House inspected the Arms which are in the Armory and found them as follows, Vizt.

1203 Guns with Bayonets.
510 without Bayonets.
12 Given by Edward Richards Esqr.
154 Cutlasses.
4 Halberts.
638 Cartouch Boxes.
37 Spare Bayonets.
4 pistols. In good Order.
25 Indian Trading Guns
and 2 Musquets not fit for service[186]

Later inventories include two *"Buckaniers"* given by Edward Richards.[187] Although Buccaneer guns were typically French naval muskets favored in the Caribbean, they were in limited use in North America and some found their way into English colonies through capture and purchase. Some French ships were required by law to carry Buccaneer muskets to various colonial ports.[188] Buccaneer muskets featured a heavy club butt and a barrel *"of an uncommon length."*[189] These were thought by some to give these cumbersome arms increased range over shorter-barreled muskets. Official contracts stipulated barrel lengths from 48 to 60 inches with both iron and brass mounts.[190]

[186] from *Colonial Records of SC; Journal of the Commons House of Assembly, 1752 – 1754.*
[187] *Ibid.*, 1757 – 1761. March 18, 1758. page 134.
[188] *The Fusil de Tulle in New France*, page 19.
[189] *Captain John Knox's Journal*. July 1, 1759. page 394.
[190] *The Fusil de Tulle in New France*. page 20.

Dutch bayonet, c. 1710 – 1730.
Private collection

As the martial spirit soared through the colony a *"Military Club"* was formed which *"appointed some of their Members to wait upon the Governor, to solicit the Use of some Public Arms, that they might learn the Bayonet Exercise; we are informed that His Excellency received their Application with his usual Condescension, applauded their Public Spirit, and was pleased to assure them, that nothing in his Power should be wanting, to promote their attaining a Proficiency in Military Exercises. This Club now consists of about 80 Members, and exercises every Thursday Afternoon, on the parade near Mr. Linds House in Ansonborough."*[191]

The Assembly paid for the importation of *"light Musquets, with Bayonets, to be sold, at Prime-Cost"* to the militia.[192] Although the maker of these light muskets remains a mystery, Wilson of London is a possibility, given the 1744 purchase of the same sort of arms and the comparative light weight of Wilson's muskets in this period. Edmond Ellinger advertised he had in his possession *"A VERY GOOD GUN,...Wilson's Make"* that had been lost.[193]

As the war dragged on, the need for a provincial establishment grew and a regiment was raised. Years of British mismanagement, bickering amongst the governments of the southern colonies, the influence of the French, and conflicts with back-country settlers finally started an all out war with a tribe that had been friendly to British interests for years, the Cherokee.

---

[191] August 18, 1757. *The Pennsylvania Gazette*.

[192] *South Carolina Commons Journal, 1755 – 1757*. page 389.

[193] *South Carolina Gazette*. August 30, 1760.

American Weapons of the French and Indian War

Left
Brass Dutch side plate.
Recovered from the site of Fort Ticonderoga.
Collection of the Fort Ticonderoga Museum

Brass mounted Dutch musket, c. 1730 – 1745.
Overall length: 60 3/4", barrel length: 46", caliber: .77.
Robert Nittolo collection

As part of the preparations for the campaign of 1760 *"Upwards of 400 provincial arms were delivered out to the militia and regulars."*[194] This inclusion of *"regulars"* may refer in part to the *"officers servants and waggoners, who were armed before we left Fort prince-George"* from a letter dated July 2, 1760.[195] In addition, rifles may have seen some limited use amongst the South Carolina provincials; *"with a few rifles from the Rangers or provincials, been fully sufficient for this purpose..."*[196] Rifles were readily available in Charleston, *"John Dod, Gunmaker"* advertised *"neat rifle barrel guns, from 3 to 4 feet in length"* for sale in his shop on Meeting Street.[197] Two years later, Dodd advertised that he had imported from London *"a neat parcel of three-square bayonets with hollow blades, from 10 to 12 inches...sockets fit to any gun."*[198]

Barrel stamp indicates South Carolina ownership.

South Carolina Rangers

In order to augment the provincial infantry establishment of South Carolina, legislation was passed on July 13, 1759 to provide funds for two mounted troops of Rangers. They would provide their own horses, provisions, and equipment.[199] Although these Rangers were *"well acquainted with the woods..."*[200] and appear to have been at least partially armed with *"a few rifles"*[201] they did not seem to be well-acquainted with military discipline. The January 17, 1760 edition of the Boston Weekly News Letter reported that *"the rifle barrel Men continue to desere [desert] 10 and 12 at a Time."*

[194] *Boston Post Boy.* January 21, 1760.
[195] *Some Observations...*
[196] *Some Observations...*
[197] *South Carolina Gazette.* November 4, 1756, Numb. 1165.
[198] *Ibid.*, November 3, 1758. Numb. 1255.
[199] *C.O.* 556. page 597 – 598.
[200] *Some Observations...*
[201] *Ibid.*

American Weapons of the French and Indian War

Brass Dutch butt plate fragment
in the archeological collection of Fort Ticonderoga.
Collection of the Fort Ticonderoga Museum

An account which described conditions with the Army under Colonel James Grant *"...Contained in the Weekly Gazette of the 16th of July...June 24, 1760... the night before our march ABOUT FORTY rangers deserted, which with not only their own horses, but a GREAT MANY MORE, which occasioned a distress in carrying on the flour-bags..."*[202]

According to an anonymous eighteenth-century author from South Carolina, this was occasioned by service under Colonel Grant and the commandeering of their horses for the pack train which gave *"some of the Rangers time and occasion to cool, be disgusted, and desert..."*[203] Those unhorsed Rangers who stayed with Grant's army were ridiculed by the British regulars as they preferred *"...taking to trees...to fight in their own way, the Indian manner"* while the Highlanders were commended in the July 16, 1760 issue of the CHARLES-TOWN Weekly Gazette[204] for receiving *"the fire of the Indians, LOOKING THEM BOLDLY IN THE FACE, with Shouldered arms, and with as little concern seemingly, as ever you saw a centinel on his post by a town-guard...however they galled us a little with their rifles, of which they seemed to be possessed of a considerable number..."*[205]

---

[202] *Some Observations...*

[203] *Ibid.*

[204] as quoted in *Some Observations...* page 81.

[205] *Some Observations...*

Another participant, possibly of the carbine-armed Highlanders or light infantry[206] had a different take on this arms disparity: *"It is a great error that the Indians ever were furnished with rifled barrelled guns, for what we suffered was chiefly owing to that cause; they wounded our men at such a distance as our carbines could scarcely do execution."*[207] In addition to arms required for the Cherokee campaign, ordnance records also include an order dated November, 21, 1763 for *"200 Musquets with Wooden Rammers, 200 Cartouch Boxes with Frogs & Belts...to be delivered...for use of the French Protestants going to Settle in the Province of South Carolina..."*[208]

---

[206] W.O. 34/70.
[207] Letter dated "Camp at Ninety-six, July 9, 1760" from the New York Gazette August 11, 1760.
[208] W.O. 47/62. page 202.

The side plate is an American made replacement.

English commercial musket, c. 1750 – 1760,
with working life additions of a 19th century lock, side plate and early barrel.
Giles and Carolyn Cromwell collection

Virginia 1750 barrel marking.
Giles and Carolyn Cromwell collection

Virginia

Virginia established a magazine in its capital quite early, first at Jamestown then at Williamsburg, to store and protect public arms and munitions. An inventory[209] of "Stores of War at Williamsburg" dated July 12, 1750, lists 364 muskets, bayonets & cartouch boxes in the Magazine, as well as 276 muskets and 100 *"Carabines"* in the Governor's House. The above stores must have been deemed lacking, as The Executive Journals of the Council of Virginia details a November 6, 1750 request that:

"the Receiver General send for from England five Hundred Muskets (to be mark't with Virginia 1750) Bayonets and Catouch Boxes of the best sort, Thirty Barrels of Cannon Powder, and Ten of Single F Two Tons of Musket Ball, and Ten Thousand Flints."[210]

The use of these arms by Virginia provincials is confirmed by a April 12, 1754 description of deserters from Alexandria, they *"...took their arms with them, having Virginia, 1750 engraved on the Barrels."*[211] Also in an inventory dated 27 September, 1757: *"goods supposed to be felloniously Stolen from His Majesty King George...At the widow Fitzpatricks'- 1 musket barrel marked (Virginia 1750)..."*[212]

---

[209] *PRO C/O 5-1338 f.53.*

[210] *Executive Journals*, Volume 5. November 1739 – May 1754. page 344.

[211] *Maryland Gazette.* April 18, 1754.

[212] *George Washington papers*. Library Of Congress Manuscript Division.

Birmingham proof marks with the FG of Farmer and Galton on the Virginia 1750 barrel.

An 1815 dated Virginia manufactory lock was added to this musket in the 19th century.

A single barrel from one of these arms survives in a private collection and although not a complete weapon, it can tell us quite a bit about these arms. The barrel is forty five and seven-eighths inches long, eighty caliber, with *"Virginia 1750"* markings. It has Birmingham proof marks, along with the *"FG"* maker's mark of the Farmer and Galton firm. Farmer and Galton of Birmingham, England, were prominent arms manufacturers, operating in one incarnation or another for a large portion of the eighteenth century. Although the barrel is marked with the FG mark, it is in no way certain that Farmer and Galton made the entire musket. Like many other contemporary gun makers, Farmer and Galton likely sold gun components as well as complete arms.

Other period correspondence indicates this was not the only purchase of commercial arms by Virginia. In addition to the original commercial purchase in 1750, and the arms from Royal Stores, Lt. Governor Dinwiddie wrote to New York's Governor James DeLancey on May 19, 1755, that he had recently imported *"from Londo., [London] 30 chests contain'g 600 stand of arms and their proper Accoutrem'ts…They do not belong to the King, but to y's Dom'n, and purchased with their own Money."*

Benjamin Roger's Horn dated 1758 and 1763. Rogers served in Andrew Lewis' company of the Virginia Regiment in 1757.
Wallace Gusler Collection

A 19th century side plate rests in the mortise.

Hanover County (Virginia) military fusee, c. 1750 – 1775.
Overall length: 54 1/2", barrel length: 38 1/2", caliber: .71.
Giles and Carolyn Cromwell collection

A private collection contains a musket possibly imported for the war. The barrel is marked *"Hanover County Virginia No. 73."* This is significant since the revised Virginia militia regulations passed in 1755 stipulated that in case any militia man was too poor to afford his own arms each county was *"to depute some person to send for the same [arms] to England...which arms so to be sent for shall be marked with the name of the county."*[213]

In a letter from Whitehall dated July 5, 1754, Sir Thomas Robinson, Secretary of State, wrote Lt. Governor Dinwiddie that *"I am now to acquaint you, that in addition to the advances of money, that are mentioned in my other Letter to you, of this Date the King has been please to order 2,000 Stands of arms with their proper Accoutrements, to be issued out of his Royal Stores, and to be deliver'd to you, by Mr. Dobbs who goes by this occasion to North Carolina and who has here received the said Arms, together with 1,000 stands for the Use of his Government..."*[214]

As previously noted, these arms were described as *"Dutch Musquets with Bayonets bought in Holland in 1741 which are of a pattern quite different from those now Issued to his Majesty's Forces here."*[215] These included cutlasses as well as the cartouch boxes and slings. A large portion of these muskets were then loaned out for the 1755 campaign; *"...I sent the Gen'l [Braddock], N. York and the Jerseys 1,700 Stand of Arms, so y't our Magazine is quite exhausted."*[216]

These muskets of *"Dutch Fabrick"* were evidently not of the highest quality: *"a Copy of a late Memorial to me from the Field Officers of both those Regiments (50th and 51st), representing the bad Condition of the Arms and Accoutrements of the Soldiers (many of which are unserviceable) and further to acquaint You that the Arms sent the last Year to the Govr. Of Virginia, part of which he lent to the provincial Troops of New York and New Jerseys, are equally bad; insomuch, that the general bad Character, which at present prevails by this means in the Colonies, of his Majesty's Arms, will, besides the other ill Consequences, which may arise to his Troops in Action, prejudice his Service here, if not rectify'd."*[217]

---

[213] *Henings' Statutes*, volume 6. 29 August, 1755. page 532.
[214] *W.O.* 34/71. page 35 – 37.
[215] 22 June, 1754. *W.O.* 47/43. page 373.
[216] Dinwiddie to Dobbs, August 29, 1755. *Dinwiddie Papers*. page 181.
[217] Shirley to Sir Thomas Robinson. September 28, 1755. *PRO CO* 5/46.

This light musket has been fitted with a Dutch lock during it's working life.

Following the complete collapse and withdrawal of Braddock's army, an emergency infusion of Sea Service arms came by way of Admiral Boscawen for the defense of Virginia. Lt. Governor Dinwiddie wrote General Shirley on October 31, 1755 that he *"...rec'd a L'r two Days ago from Adm'l Boscawen, dated 11th Sept'r, with 500 bbls. Gun Powder and 400 small Arms, w'ch were much wanted here, having very little of either in our magazine."*

Listed as *"Bright Arms"* with cartouch boxes, bayonets, belts and frogs, their hardware was polished. Some sea service muskets in this period were finished *"Black"* in an effort to retard rust. An account delivered by Edward Boscawen to the Board of Ordnance dated March 6, 1756,[218] notes the muskets came in quantities of 50 from the ships *Torbay, Monarch, Yarmouth, Chichester, Somerset, Northumberland* and *Grafton*. The vessels Anson and Nottingham each gave out 25 stands along with powder in varying quantities.

Additional arms were requested from *"Mr. Turner, Comptroller of the Ordnance in Boston"* by Governor Dinwiddie, who noted that the 1,000 stands were *"to ret'n the same at the expiration of the Expedit'n to H.M'y's Stores at Boston, unless taken or destroy'd by the Enemy."*[219]

On May 24th, Dinwiddie alerted Governor and General Shirley that *"I have sent a Sloop for the Arms, &c., with an Order from the Council here to return them to the Magazine at Boston at the end of the Expedition."*[220] These arms must have arrived in less than pristine condition as Dinwiddie's letter to Lord Loudon of October 28th, 1756, indicated that *"One Thousand of the Arms included in the Store-keeper's Acco't transmitted Yo. Were sent me from Boston in a very rusty Condition, and it w'd appear they had been under Water for Months. I've emply'd Smiths to clean and put 'em in the best Order they can."*[221]

---

[218] *W.O.* 55/355. page 240.

[219] Dinwiddie to Turner, May 21st, 1756. *Dinwiddie papers*.

[220] Dinwiddie to Shirley, May 24th, 1756. *Ibid*.

[221] Dinwiddie to Loudon, October 28th, 1756. *Ibid*., page 532.

Given the date and the origin of the shipment, these arms were most likely part of the 10,000 stands of Long Land muskets sent to Shirley the winter prior. During this time, the Virginia provincials also began using powder horns with and without cartridge boxes. Colonel Washington instructed Captain Thomas Waggener *"I desire you will take care to have each man of your command furnished with powder-horns and shot-bags."*[222]

Other unknown commercial purchases or confiscation may account for the inclusion of a small amount of Buccaneer muskets in colony's stores. *"An Exact Return of Cloathing, Arms, Ammunition &c. at Fort Loudon Belonging to the Virginia Regiment for October 25th, 1757"*[223] lists an inventory of *"10 Buckaneers"* along with *"298 Muskets wantg Repair,"* *"328 Muskets Broke"* as well as *"253 Stands of Arms."* The Virginia Regiment was impressing arms as they grew scarce in Virginia:

Thurs. May 12 , 1757

It appears to us, that Samuel Cobbs, Gent. Lieutenant of the County of Amelia, furnished the Men draughted out of that County, at his own expence, with 22 Muskets, with Bayonets and Cartouche boxes, and other Accoutrements, and 22 cutting swords, amounting in the whole to £78,12s,6d which were detained by Col. Washington, for the Use of the Virginia Regiment, and that the same Samuel Cobbs hath not received any Satisfaction for the same. Resolved that it is the Opinion of this Commitee, that the said Samuel Cobbs ought to be allowed the said Sum of £78,12s,6d. to be paid by the public."[224]

---

[222] Washington to Waggener, September 6, 1756. *George Washington papers.*

[223] *George Washington Papers.* Library of Congress.

[224] *Journal of the House of Burgesses, 1752 – 58.* page 463.

The shallow mortise indicates this gun may have been fitted with a convex side plate of the same size as contemporary carbines.

Unlike the soldiers from other colonies, regimental returns from this period indicate that the sergeants of the regiment were being equipped with swords. A document entitled *"An Exact Return of Cloathing, Arms, Ammunition &c. at Fort Loudon Belonging to the Virginia Regiment for October 25th, 1757"*[225] lists both swords and sashes in a section of the inventory entitled *"serjeant's clothing."* Given the healthy supply of naval cutlasses in Virginia during this period, that form is a strong candidate for the issue sergeant's sword, although variants of a small sword shaped brass hanger have been excavated from numerous sites in Williamsburg, including the Governor's Palace. Washington wrote Lt. Governor Dinwiddie that *"Very few of the Draughts have arms; I have several Smiths employed in repairing the old ones in store here, which can scarcely be made serviceable. They can not be completed with Bayonets and cartouch-boxes. It was not 'till lately, I have been able to procure an Armourer; although I had used my best endeavoours to do so these 8 months past."*[226]

As a second battalion of Virginians under Colonel William Byrd III was raised to assist the Forbes expedition, arms and accouterments were in even greater demand. With no sure supply in hand from Britain, Washington requested supplies from his government as well as continuing to repair existing arms. Colonel Henry Bouquet forwarded orders to Washington that stated *"The Col. Is desired to collect in Virginia as many Powder horns as can be got, all that can be had from Pensilvania shall be ordered…For Shot Pouches, osnabrug [a course, unbleached and cheap linen] will be bought, with thread to make them one yard will make 8 bags."*[227]

Detail of guard

British authorities scrambled to cobble munitions together for Crown forces and, without the expected arms shipment from the Tower, were forced to get them in the colonies. Following protracted bickering between acting Virginia Governor and President of the Council John Blair and British Quartermaster Sir John St. Clair in May, 700 arms from Virginia which were *"all the Arms in the Magazine, and all those in the Governor's House…"* were packed up for the campaign.[228] Given the tardiness of the expected arms shipment, St. Clair seems to have been hedging his bets by simultaneously requesting arms from both the colony of Virginia and Maryland, which had declined to pay for a regiment for the campaign.

---

[225] *George Washington Papers*. Library of Congress.

[226] Washington to Dinwiddie. July 10, 1757. *Ibid.*

[227] Bouquet to Washington. June 13, 1758. George *Ibid.*, page 208.

[228] Executive Journals of Virginia Council 6:96 – 99 as quoted in *Washington papers, Colonial Series* Volume 5, page 212.

Small sword style English infantry hanger, c. 1720 – 1750.
Private collection

St. Clair wrote Forbes that *"I shall get Govr Sharpe [of Maryland] to send up to Frederick Town 700 arms that I may have them at Hand; but I shall not mention this untill Colo Washington is gone, lest it should stop Mr. Blair sending those which are at Williamsburg."*[229] Governor Sharpe wrote General Forbes that *"500 new muskets...have been since sent from that place to Winchester to arm the Virginia Forces..."*[230] Meanwhile, Washington received orders from Henry Bouquet on June 13th that stated *"No Arms are to be taken from Maryland. I hope the Col. will be able to arm the two Regimts and the Militia Compa: in having the arms in Stores repaired..."*[231] St. Clair also wrote Colonel Washington on the same day noting *"...you will receive near 700 arms for the 2d Virginia Regiment from Williamsburg, you are to take into your Store at Winchester the Maryland Arms which were deliverd to the 2d Regiment, these Arms are to be deliverd to Govr Sharpe on his Order."*[232] Washington replied that *"There will be a difficency of Bayonets when the Maryland Arms are returned; and there is not a possibility of my supplying Byrds Regiment with Cartooch Boxes, as the arms which Mr. Henry is repairing are entirely without these Appendiges. My regiment will I expect, be compleat in both these articles."*[233]

Washington cautioned that *"Colo. Byrd will be sadly distress'd for Arms when those from Maryland are deliver'd up. The Arms from Williamsburg came here in such bad Order, that they cannot possibly be repair'd in time; Colo. Byrd writes to you on this subject himself, it will therefore be needless for me to enlarge upon or repeat His complaints."*[234] The same day,[235] Byrd's letter to Forbes dated June 23, 1758 expounds on the issue: *"I have been a good deal puzzled about arming my Men, but have at last done it compleatly by picking the Muskets & c. which came from Williamsburgh & Maryland. Sr John St Clair has orderd me to return the Maryland arms & to take the remainder of the Williamsburgh arms in the room of them; I have consulted the Armorer who says he does not think the old Guns, (about 320) are fit for Service, for they have been in the Magazeen below ever since the Reign of King William* [Byrd's assertion was an exaggeration. The Magazine in Williamsburg was built in 1715 by Governor Spotswood, thirteen years after the death of King William in 1702]. *I hope Sir you will not think I do amiss in not returning all the Maryland Arms, as in that case I shoud either be obliged to march to Fort Cumberland without that number of Guns, or dissobey Colo. Bouquets orders & wait till I coud get those you mention'd from Carlisle, which would take up a fortnight. I think it best to replace Ld [Lord] Baltimores Arms [the arms from Maryland] out of those in Carlisle."*[236]

The prickly St. Clair cautioned Forbes against providing the Virginians with the recent arms from England that Byrd had mentioned: *"You will never see more of them, for out of the great numbers that were deliver'd out to ye militia of Virginia not one of them could be found."*[237]

---

[229] St.Clair to Forbes. May 24, 1758. *Forbes Papers*, Box #4.

[230] Sharpe to Forbes. 9th June, 1758. *Ibid.*

[231] Bouquet to Washington. *Washington papers.* page 208.

[232] St. Clair to Washington. June 13, 175. *Ibid.* page 210.

[233] Washington to St. Clair. June 14, 1758. *Ibid.*

[234] Washington to Sir John St. Clair. June 23, 1758.

[235] June 24, 1758. *George Washington papers.*

[236] Byrd to Forbes. June 23, 1758. *Forbes Papers*, Box #4.

[237] St. Clair to Forbes. June 17, 1758. *Ibid.*

Small sword style English infantry hanger, c. 1720 – 1750.
Photographed with permission from
The Colonial Williamsburg Foundation

Sword fragment recovered from the
Governor's Palace in Williamsburg.
The Colonial Williamsburg Foundation

Upon receiving his orders Colonel Washington wrote to Mister *"Henry-ARMOURER…"* at Fort Loudon:

Sir;

So soon as you have completed Colo. Byrd's Regiment, and Captn. Stewarts Troop of Light Horse with Arms, you are to set about cleaning and putting all the Virginia Arms in the best repair you can, till further Orders…Such Pieces as want Locks, or in other repsects much repair, let be your last care, and when you may be call'd away you are to deliver in a faithful Acct. of all the Arms that have pas'd thro your hands, from the first of your coming, to the Store keeper Lt. Smith, and bring, or send, another Copy to me."[238]

---

[238] Washington to William Henry. June 24, 1758. *George Washington papers*, volume 5, page 240.

Right
George Washington in the Uniform of a British Colonial Colonel, c. 1772.
By Charles Willson Peale.
Washington-Custis-Lee Collection
Washington and Lee University, Lexington, Virginia.

As the two Virginia Regiments marched for Pennsylvania, Lieutenant Charles Smith was left in charge of a tiny garrison in Winchester, and his return of arms at Fort Loudon, dated July 30, 1758, lists the following Virginia arms:

160 Muskets Repaird
440 Muskets not Repaird
290 Bayonitts Repaird
250 Bayonetts Not Repaird
170 Muskets Barrels

as well as a "Chest of Muskets", "75 Carbines", 230 "Bullets Moles" from Maryland stores.[239]

This return seems to indicate that Byrd did indeed utilize some Maryland arms for the 2nd Virginia Regiment, as out of 700 total "Virginia Arms", 440 remained behind without receiving repairs.

Shortages of suitable arms continued to plague the regiment. The newly-promoted Virginia provincial commanding officer Colonel Adam Stephen sent a report to General Amherst on May 27, 1762, that *"we have no bayonets"*[240] and another dated July 9, 1762, that *"The Muskets after all the repairs I can give them will be very indifferent & I have only 250 Cartouch boxes..."*[241] Virginia received a final wartime shipment of infantry muskets from Royal Stores in New York. On October 4, 1763 Sir Jeffrey Amherst requested that *"a Thousand Stand, Consisting of Muskets, Bayonets, and Cartouch Boxes...of the Pattern which you have already Shewn me..."*[242] be packed up and shipped to Virginia. Sadly, no further indication of the specific pattern sent has come to light.

---

[239] *Washington papers*, page 352, note 5.

[240] *W.O.* 34/90, page 158.

[241] *W.O.* 34/91, page 31.

[242] *W.O.* 34/70, page 98.

Iron hilted English infantry hanger, c. 1750.
Private collection

Detail of blade marking.

Virginia Light Horse Arms

In addition to the four Virginia provincial infantry companies, and the two road-building companies of *"Hatchet men or carpenters"*, General Braddock also established a 34-man company (including non-commissioned officers) of *"Horse Rangers"* under Captain Robert Stewart which came to be known as the Virginia Light Horse.[243] Braddock's orders specified *"Every officer Sergeant, corporal and private to be armed with a short carbine, case of pistols and a cuttng Sword."*[244] Proper cavalry equipage was lacking, which forced Braddock to improvise: *"Capt Stewart is to Apply Immeddiately to Sr Peter Halkett [of the 44th Regiment] for 34 Hangers for his men which They are to take with Them."*[245]

From the encampment near Alexandria, Virginia, Sir Peter Halkett sent off a letter to Quarter Master St. Clair in Winchester: *"That troop has only got swords, let me know how they are to be provided with other arms and accoutrements fit for a troop, here and at Alexandria there is no leather proper to make bucketts of..."*[246] St. Clair replied the next day, adding *"I beg you would get your armourers to cut a sufficient quantity of Virginia arms for the horse Rangers..."*[247] most likely indicating that 34 of the recently arrived Dutch muskets were to be shortened for mounted use. Having procured swords and shortened muskets, the troop topped it off with Sea Service *"Pistols- Thirty Four pairs"* from the ship Centurion.[248]

---

[243] Braddock Orderly Book, entry February 28, 1755. *Braddock Road Chronicles*, page 63.
[244] *Ibid.*
[245] Halkett Orderly Book, entry April 8, 1755. *Braddock Road Chronicles*, page 117.
[246] *Braddock Road Chronicles*, dated April 16, 1755. page 136.
[247] St. Clair to Halkett, April 17, 1755. *Ibid.*, page 137.
[248] An Account of Ordnance Stores Supplied to His Excellency General Braddock for the use of the Army from His Majesty's Ships under the Command of the Honorable Augustus Kepple 1757, W.O. 55/412, page 172.

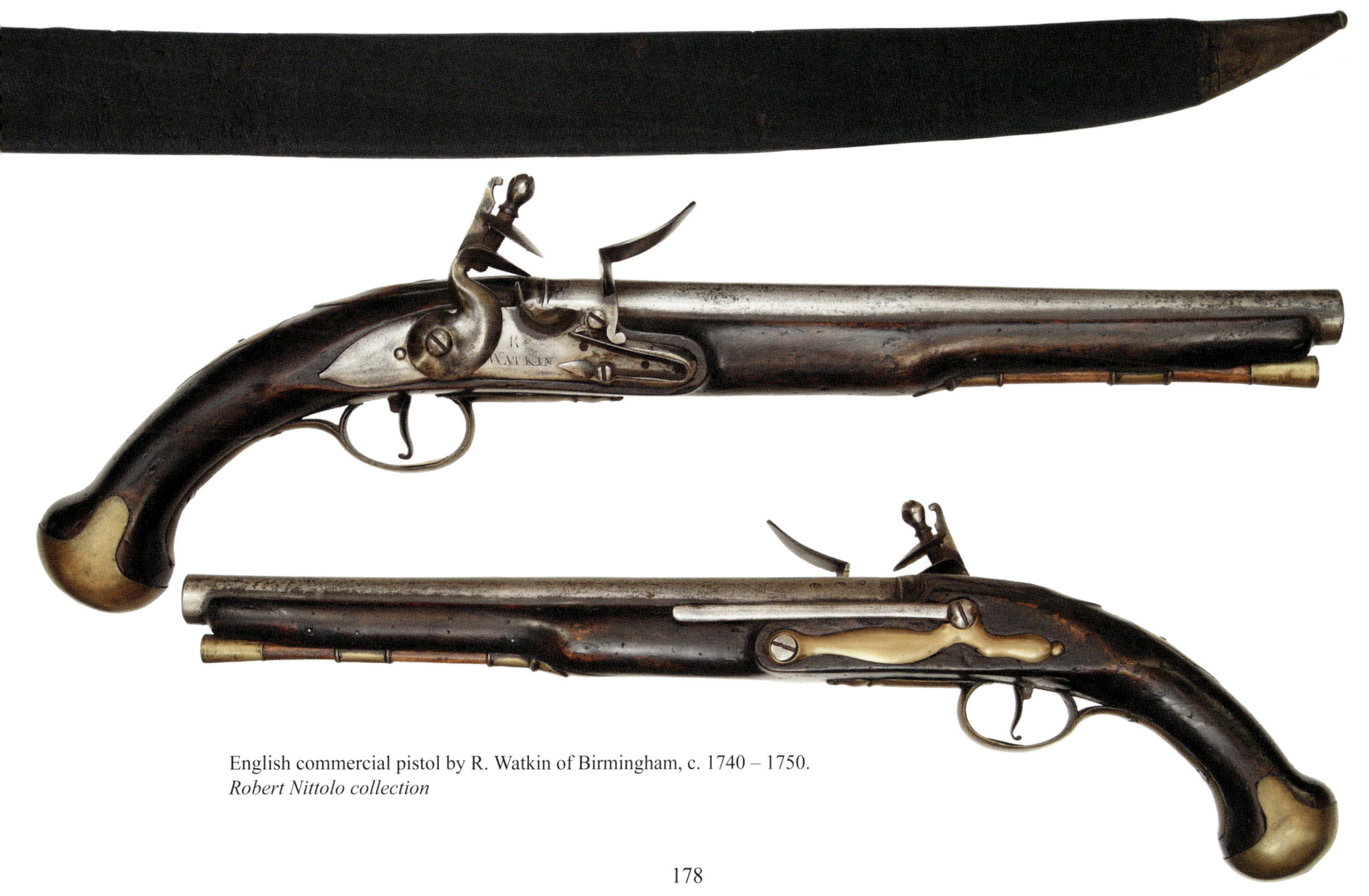

English commercial pistol by R. Watkin of Birmingham, c. 1740 – 1750.
Robert Nittolo collection

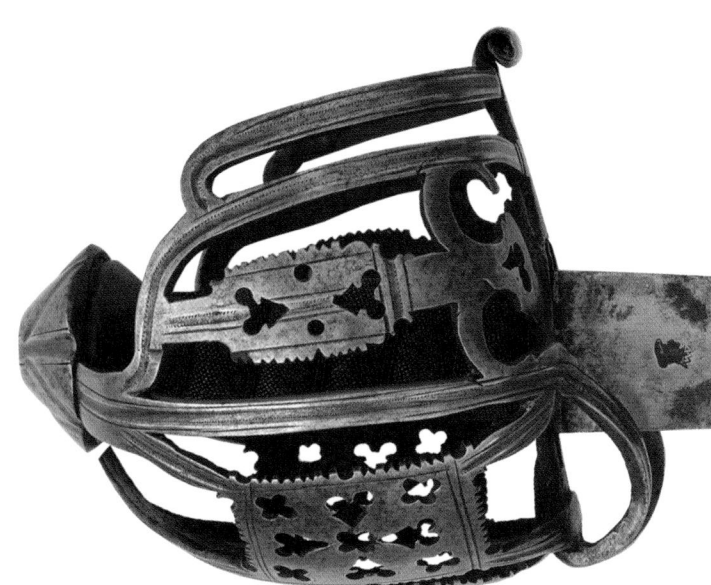

Scottish broadsword, c. 1730 – 1750.
Private collection

Discipline amongst the troop was not always strictly maintained. In a letter To Lt. Governor Robert Dinwiddie[249] Colonel George Washington wrote:

"This Morning, before we could parade the Men, to March upon the last Alarm, arrived a Second Express, ten times more terrified than the former, with information that the Indians had got within four Miles of the Town, and were killing and destroying all before them; for that he himself had heard constant Firing, and the Shrieks of the unhappy Murder'd! Upon this, I immediately collected what Force I could, which consisted of 22 Men, recruited for the Rangers, and 19 of the Militia, and Marched therewith directly to the place where these horrid Murders were said to be committed. When we came there, whom shou'd we find occasioning all this disturbance, but 3 drunken Soldiers of the Light-Horse, carousing, firing their Pistols, and uttering the most unheard-of Imprecations; these we took, and Marched Prisoners to Town, where we met the Men I sent out last Night, and learned that the party of Indians, discovered by Isaac Julian, proved to be a Mulatto and Negro, seen hunting of Cattle by his Son, who alarmed the Father, and the Father the Neighbourhood. These Circumstances are related only to shew what a panick prevails among the People; how much they are alarmed at the most usual and customary Crys; and yet how impossible it is to get them to act in any respect for their common Safety's." Despite the occasional drunken *"carousing"* the Light Horse troop must have been quite useful, but shortages in men forced the utilization of the troop to be used as garrison troops. In a letter from Colonel George Washington to Governor Dinwiddie Colonel Washington noted that *"Captain Stewart's troop has for these twelve months past, and must still continue to do duty on foot."*[250]

The troop was raised and mounted again in order to assist the Forbes expedition, using men in the 1st Virginia Regiment (a second regiment of Virginia provincials had been authorized for the campaign). On May 24, 1758, Colonel Washington wrote Lieutenant Colonel Adam Stephen who was then at Fort Loudoun Virginia:

"You are to get 40 men from the Second Regiment, to supply the places of the like number to be taken out of the First, to assist in forming a Troop of Light Horse: And, to prevent, the evil consequences of forcing men out of one Regiment into the other; you are, with Colo. Mercer (who will assist you in the undertaking) to use your best endeavours to persuade the number of men wanted, to offer themselves voluntarily."

The later incarnation of the Light Horse troop was rearmed by General Forbes in 1758 from available arms in Maryland stores. In a letter to Forbes, Governor Sharpe of Maryland noted that *"upwards of 50 old but the best Carbines that I could collect in the Province & 33 Pair of Pistols have been since sent from that place to Winchester to arm the Virginia Forces. I have likewise ordered 50 Broad swords Scabbards & Belts 40 Pair of Holsters & as many Blanketts & Shoulder Belts with Springs as can be got in Annapolis to be sent thence to Winchester."*[251]

---

[249] Winchester, October 11, 1755. *George Washington papers*.
[250] Winchester, August 4, 1756. *Ibid*.
[251] Sharpe to Forbes. 9th June, 1758. *Forbes Papers*, Box #4.

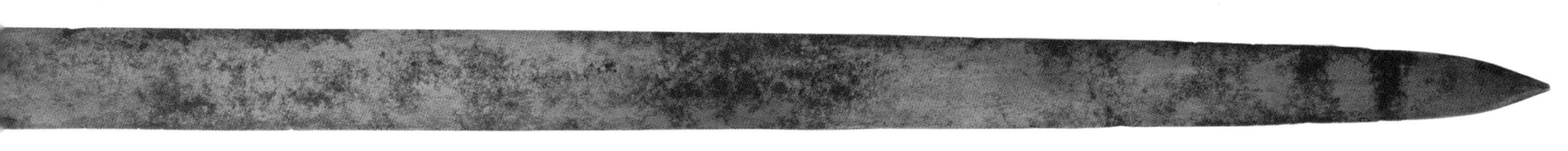

Maryland inventories from the period reflect a variety of arms from both Ordnance stores and Commercial purchases, including *"Basket Hilt Horseman's Swords...Buff Belts."* Sword hilts in wartime Maryland inventories are described as bright, black, and brass-finished. An undated basket hilted broadsword with Maryland Revolutionary War provenance is a possible example of these weapons. It is said to have been carried by Captain Nicholas Ruxton Moore of the 4th Continental Light Dragoons and is in the collections of the Maryland Historical Society.[252]

Virginia Rangers

Following the general reorganization of the colony's defenses after Braddock's defeated army withdrew to Philadelphia in 1755, Virginia also formed separate companies of Rangers (not to be confused with the uniformed provincials of the companies termed "Rangers" by Braddock during his campaign in 1755). These men were not uniformed or armed by the colony, but were paid and fed from public funds for "ranging" between frontier posts and scouting for enemy Indians.

Not everyone viewed the Rangers as an effective fighting force. Washington complained that *"the Rangers who we were told, were blocked up by the Indians in small Fortresses. But if I may offer my opinion, I believe that they were more encompassed by Fear than by the Enemy."*[253] Some of the men of the Ranging companies were armed with rifles. Sergeant Peter Luney testified that in June of 1756 he lost *"a rifle Gun of the value of Four Pounds ten Shillings"* when he was captured by a French and Indian party that destroyed Fort Vause.[254]

Conclusion

The French and Indian War, was a time of great transition for British military firearms. New designs such as the Pattern 1756 Infantry musket, the Marine or Militia musket, and various carbines were developed in reaction to lessons learned on the battlefield. A preference for lighter arms more suited for the woodlands of North America developed. The war also furthered the spread of the rifle-barreled gun in America. Even Indian tribes in the southern and middle colonies began to demand rifles in preference to the low-quality trade fusils peddled to them by English and colonial agents . Back-country settlers and some soldiers also found the rifle well suited to their needs. The vast theater destroyed older, outdated, non-standard, and poor quality arms and equipment. Although arms arrived in huge numbers, the fortunes of war, desertion, poor record-keeping and improper maintenance insured many of these arms never made it back into Royal stores. The surviving arms, as well as the expertise acquired by Americans in the provincial service would appear years later on the battlefields of the American Revolution.

---

[252] *Peterson's Arms and Armor in Colonial America,* page 258, plate 250.

[253] Washington to Dinwidde, October 11, 1755. *Washington papers.*

[254] Friday, April 7th, 1758. *Journals of the House of Burgesses of Virginia*, page 502.

Of Sorts For Provincials

Tower of London, seen from the river, with a view of Traitors Gate, photo by Viki Male

State the Small Arms and Appurtenances in Store at the Tower for Land and Sea Services 31 December 1754. WO 47/45

[Note: This is only the portion dealing with long arms]

Extraordinary Musquets 100 (Servble)

Land Musquets to the Kings Pattern with double bridle Locks

Long With Steel Rammers

With New Pattern Nosebands Bayoneted 4,623
With Old Ditto do. 636
Without Nosebands do. 307 (Servble.) 166 (To Clean) 32 (To Clean & Repair)
800 (Rough Stocked)

Long With Wood Rammers

With Old Pattern Nosebands Bayoneted 1,508 Without do. 1374
Without Nosebands Bayoneted 21243 Without Do. 30,160 (Servble.)
618 (To Clean) 696 (To Clean & Repair) 382 (Rough Stocked)

Short with Wood Rammers

With new Pattern Nosebands- Bayoneted 1,408
With Old Do. Do. 583 Without Nosebands do. 8,408 (Servbl.) 6 (To Clean)
105 (To Clean & Repair) 10 (To New Stock) 267 (Rough Stocked)

Musquets for Land or Sea Service

With Single Bridle Locks-do 343, 54, 1,090, 71,"
Marine New Pattern do 6,108, ", 215, ", "
Marine Old Pattern do. 352, ", 884, 100, "
Dutch with brass Furniture Bayoneted 641 (Servbl.)
Without do [without bayonets] 72, 1,148, 3267, 528
Spanish wth Iron Furniture Bayoneted 241, ", 878, 450, "

Sea Service Muskets of Sorts

With bright Barrels & brass Furniture Tower Proof
Bayoneted 679, 540, 2948, 75, "
With do. Made by the Trade without do. 435, 298, 16, 7, "
With black Barrels & brass Furniture Bayonetted 840 (Servbl.)
Without Do. [without bayonets] 4,016, 341, 1,059, 94, "
Of Sorts with Iron Furniture do. ", 64, 362, ", "

Totals of Musquets

84,277 [Serv.ble or Serviceable]
3,235 [To Clean]
11,552 [To Clean & Repair]
1,717 [To Rough Stock]
1,067 [Rough Stock'd]

State of Arms to be kept in Store at the Tower 9 September, 1757. WO 47/46

Long land Musquets with Steel Rammers & Long fore pipes 50,000
Short land Musquets with Woodrammers for Dragoons 10,000
Short Musquets of the New Pattern for Marines or Militia 30,000
Carbines with Bayonets for Artillery or Highlanders 50,000
Carbines without Bayonets for Horse 2,000
Land Service Pistols Pairs 12,000
Sea Service Muskets wth Bayonets Bright 10,000 Black 10,000
Musquettoons 2,000
Sea Service Pistols pairs 10,000

American Weapons of the French and Indian War

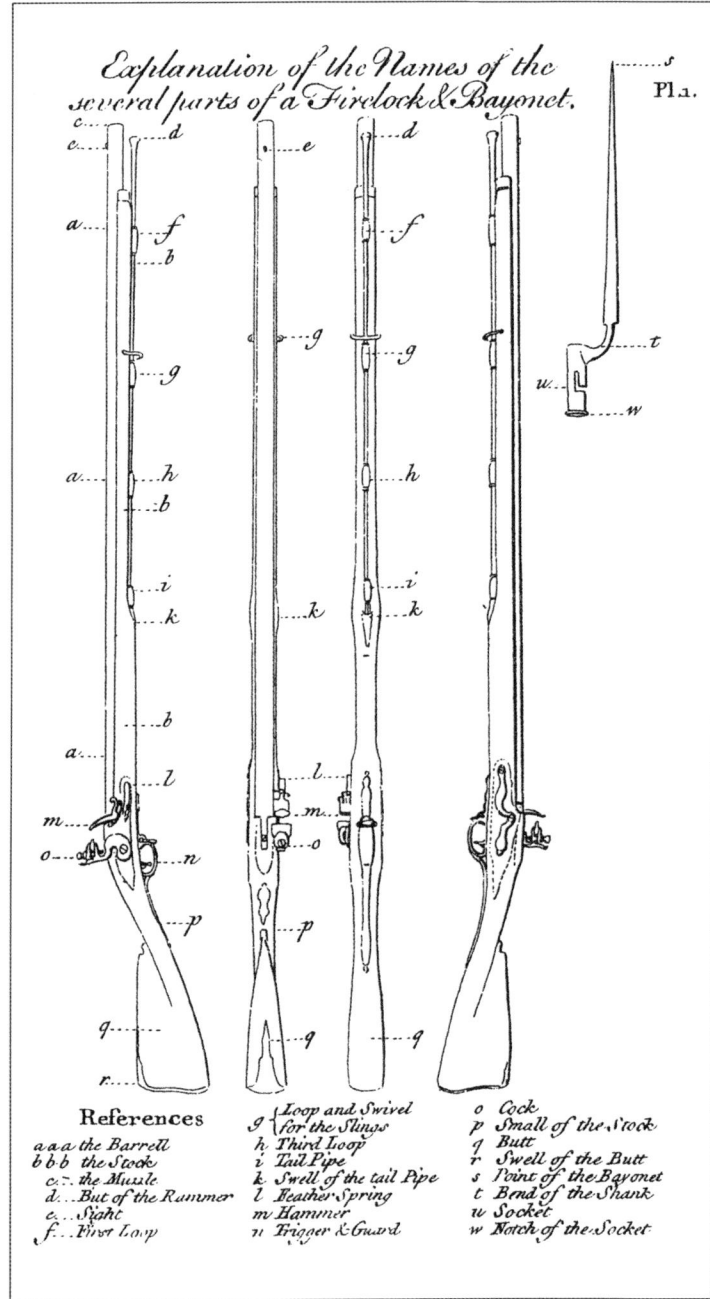

Windham, William. *A plan of discipline, composed for the use of the militia of the County of Norfolk.* London, 1759. Plate 1.
Private collection

Glossary

Note: all of the Definitions included in the Glossary come from *The Gentleman's Compleat Military Dictionary* printed in 1759.

CARABINE [Carbine]: is a Fire Arm, shorter than a Firelock, and it carries a Ball of 24 in the Pound [British carbines of the period generally fired a ball measuring approximately .615" diameter]; they are carried by the Light Horse, hanging at a Belt over the left Shoulder.

CARTRIDGE is a Case of Pastboard or Parchment [as well as whitish brown paper], containing the exact Charge of a Fire Arm; those for Musquets, Carabines or Pistols, hold both the Powder and Ball for the Charge.

CARTRIDGE-BOX [also frequently termed "Cartouch" Box, not to be confused with the contemporary Cartridge "Pouch" which was slung from the shoulder instead of the Cartridge "Box" which was carried on a waist belt] is a Case of Wood, or turn'd Iron covered with Leather [the cartridge boxes issued from the Tower featured a wooden block with 9, 12, 18 or 24 holes, those with "turn'd Iron" or tin tubes seem to have been privately procured items as there is no indication of such in contemporary Tower inventories. Examples of the tin tube boxes can be seen in contemporary portraits of British Officers], holding a dozen Musquet Cartridges; it is wore upon a Belt, and hangs a little higher than the right Pocket-Hole.

COMPTROLLER of the Artillery, inspects the Musters of the Artillery, makes the Pay-List, take the Accompts and Remains of Stores, and is accountable to the Office of Ordnance.

FIRE-LOCK, is a Fire Arm carried by a Foot Soldier; The Barrel of it is about three Foot eight inches long, the Stock about four Foot and eight Inches, and the Bore is fit to receive a Bullet of Lead of an ounce weight [British musket bores generally utilized a ball measuring 0.69" diameter].

MUSQUET, [or 'Musket'; also see 'Fire-Lock' usually a full size smooth bore gun] is the most commodious and useful Fire-Arm used in the Army...

ORDINANCE, all sorts of Guns, Mortars, Firelocks, Carabins, Pistols, &c. all sorts of Arms or Stores...

[Cartridge] POUCH; a Grenadier's Pouch, is a square Case or Bag of Leather, with a Flap over it, hanging in a Strap of about two Inches broad, over the left Shoulder...

Bibliography

Abbot, W.W., ed. *The Papers of George Washington.* Charlottesville: University Press, 1988 Colonial Series 5 volumes.

Ahearn, Bill. *Muskets in the American Revolution and Other Colonial Wars.* Lincoln, RI.: Andrew Mobray Inc, 2005.

Andrews, Frank D. *Connecticut Soldiers in the French and Indian War Bills, Receipts and Documents.* Vineland, New Jersey: 1925.

Anonymous. *The Gentleman's Compleat Military Dictionary.* Boston: 1759.

Bailey, DeWitt. *British Military Flintlock Rifles. 1740 – 1840.* Lincoln, RI.: Andrew Mobray Inc, 2002.

Pattern Dates for British Ordnance Small Arms 1718 – 1783. Gettysburg, Pa.: Thomas Publications, 1997.

The Wilsons: Gunmakers to Empire 1730 – 1832. American Society of Arms Collector's Bulletin, Printed by Science Press Division Ephrata, Pennsylvania, 2002.

Blackmore, Howard, L. *British Military Firearms.* London: Herbert Jenkins LTD, 1961.

Dutch Muskets for Ireland, 1706 – 1715. Arms Collecting, Vol. 32, No. 3 (Aug. 1994).

Gunmakers of London, 1350 – 1850. York, Pa. George Shumway, 1986.

Bouton, Nathanial, ed. Provincial Papers, *Documents and Records relating to the Province of New-Hampshire,* Volume VI. Manchester: 1872

Bradley, Robert L. and Camp, Helen B. *The Forts of Pemaquid, Maine: An Archaeological and Historical Study.* Augusta, Maine: Maine Historic Preservation Commission, 1994.

Brock, R.A., ed. *The Official Records of Robert Dinwiddie, Lieutenant Governor of the Colony of Virginia, 1751-1758.* New York: AMS Press, 1971. 2 volumes.

Bouchard, Russel. *The Fusil de Tulle in New France 1691 – 1741.* Bloomfield, ON Canada: Museum Restoration Service, 1998.

Cardwell, John M. *Mismanagement: the 1758 British Expedition Against Carillon.* Fort Ticonderoga Museum Bulletin, Volume XV, 1992, #4.

Clarke, John B. *The State of New Hampshire: Miscellaneous Provincial Papers 1725 – 1800.* Manchester, New Hampshire: 1898.

Colonial Williamsburg Foundation. *Notes on Williamsburg Magazine, Ordinance and Types of Uniforms used prior to Revolution.* CWF Library Research Report Series, Unpublished., Williamsburg, Virginia.

Connecticut. *The Public Records of the Colony of Connecticut, from April 1636 to October 1776...transcribed and published, (in accordance with a resolution of the General assembly).* Hartford: Brown & Parsons, 1850 – 1890. 15 vols.

Forbes Papers. *General John Forbes Headquarters Papers.* Alderman Library Manuscript Collection, University of Virginia. Unpublished

Fort Ticonderoga. *Fort Ticonderoga Bulletin,* Volume 2, #2, July 1930. New York, USA.

Furnis Letterbook. *James Furnis Letterbook 1755 – 1758.* Clements Library Manuscript Collection. Unpublished.

Fitch, Thomas. *The Fitch Papers Correspondence and Documents during Thomas Fitch's Governorship of the Colony of Connecticut 1754 – 1766.* Hartford:Connecticut Historical Society, 1918. Volume I.

Georgia. *Colonial Records of the State of Georgia.* Atlanta, Ga: Franklin Printing and Publishing Company, 1904.

Goldstein, Erik. *The Socket Bayonet in the British Army.* Lincoln, Rhode Island: Mowbray Publishers 2000.

Grimm, Jacob. *Archaeological Investigation of Fort Ligonier.* Pittsburg Pennsylvania, USA: Carnegie Museum, 1970.

Hall, Wilmer L., ed. *Executive Journals of the Council of Colonial Virginia,* Volume V (November 1, 1739 – May 7, 1754). Richmond, Virginia, USA: Virginia State Library 1967.

Hamilton, Milton,W., ed. *The papers of Sir William Johnson.* Albany: University of the State of New York, 1921 – 1965.

Haynes, George Henry, Rice, Franklin P., Tillinghast, Cabeb B. and Corey, Deloraine P. eds. *Transactions and Collections of the American Antiquarian Society: Manuscript Records of the French and Indian war in the Library of the Society,* Volume XI. Worcester, Massachusetts: American Antiquarian Society, 1909.

Hazard, Samuel. *Pennsylvania Archives Selected and Arranged from Original Documents in the Office of the Secretary of the Commonwealth, Conformably to Acts of the General Assembly.* Philadelphia, PA.: Joseph Severns & Co., 1853.

Hening, William Waller, ed. *The Statutes at large; being a collection of all the laws of Virginia, from the first session of the Legislature in the year 1619.* Charlottesville Virginia, USA: University Press of Virginia, 1969.

Henry, David. *An historical description of the Tower of London and its curiosities.* London: 1753.

James, Alfred Procter, Ph.D., ed. *Writings of General John Forbes Relating to his Service in North America.* Menasha, Wisconsin: The Collegiate Press, 1938.

Knox, John D. (Doughty, Arthur G. Ed.). *An historical journal of the campaigns in North America for the years 1757, 1758 and 1760 Volumes I-III.* Toronto Canada: Champlain Society, 1914 – 1916.

Labaree, L. W. Ketcham, R.L. Boatfield, H. C. Fineman, H. H. eds. *Papers of Benjamin Franklin,* Volume 6: April 1, 1755 through September 24, 1756. Yale University Press, USA, 1963.

Lincoln, Charles Henry, ed. *Correspondence of William Shirley Governor of Massachusetts and Military Commander in America 1731 – 1760.* New York: The MacMillan Company, 1912.

Lipscomb, Terry, ed. *Colonial Records of South Carolina; Journal of the Commons House of Assembly 1752 – 1754.* Columbia, South Carolina, USA: University of South Carolina Press, 1983.

Lipscomb, Terry, ed. *Colonial Records of South Carolina; Journal of the Commons House of Assembly 1755 – 1757.* Columbia, South Carolina, USA: University of South Carolina Press, 1989.

Colonial Records of South Carolina; Journal of the Commons House of Assembly 1757 – 1761. Columbia, South Carolina, USA: South Carolina Department of Archives and History, 1996.

Massachusetts Archives Collection. *unpublished MS.*

Massachusetts Historical Society. *Journals of the House of Representatives of Massachusetts.* Volumes XXXIII, XXXIV and XXXV. Portland Maine, USA: 1960-1963.

McIlwaine, H.R., ed. *Journals of the House of Burgesses of Virginia 1752 – 1755 1756 – 1758.* Richmond, Virginia USA: 1909.

Moller, George. *American Military Shoulder Arms*, Vol. 1.

Mulligan Robert E. *City of New York Muskets of 1755 – 1775.* Man at Arms Magazine, Volume 13, No. 2, March/April, 1991.

Neumann, George. *Battle Weapons of the American Revolution.* Texarkana, Texas: Scurlock Publishing 1998.

Neumann, George and Kravic, Frank. *Collector's Illustrated Encyclopedia of the American Revolution.* Texarkana, Texas: Scurlock Publishing 1975.

New York Historical Society. Quarterly Bulletin, Vol. XXIII No. 1. New York, USA: January 1939.

Norreys, Jephson O'Conor, ed. *Servant of the Crown, In England and in North America, 1756-1761 Based upon the papers of John Appy, Secretary and Judge Advocate of His Majesty's Forces.* Published by the Society of Colonial Wars in the State of New York. New York, USA: D. Appleton Century Company, 1938.

Pargellis, Stanley, ed. *Military Affairs in North America - Selected documents from the Cumberland Papers in Windsor Castle.* USA: Archon Books, 1969.

Pennsylvania. *Minutes of the Provincial Council From the Organization to the Termination of the Proprietary Government.* Harrisburg, PA.: Theo. Fenn and Company, 1851.

Pennsylvania Historical Society Collection. *unpublished MS.*

Peterson, Harold L. *Arms and Armor in Colonial America 1526 – 1783.* New York, USA: Bramhall House, 1956.

Philopatrios (Anonymous). *Some Observations on the Two Campaigns against the Cherokee Indians, in 1760 and 1761.* CHARLES-TOWN: Printed and Sold by Peter Timothy, MDCCLXIL.

Public Records Office. *unpublished MS.*

Rhode Island Historical Society. *Colonial Militia Collection, Richard Partridge Collection.* unpublished MS.

Saunders, William L., ed. *Colonial Records of North Carolina.* New York: AMS Press, 1968.

Skennerton, Ian D. & Richardson, Robert. *British Commonwealth Bayonets.* Margate, Australia: Skennerton Publishing 1984.

Unknown. *The Gentleman's Compleat Military Dictionary.* Boston: Edes and Gill, Green and Russell, 1759

Wahl, Andrew J. *Braddock Road Chronicles 1755.* Bowie: Maryland Heritage Books 1999.

Index

1st New York Regiment, 132

1st Pennsylvania Battalion, 143

1st Virginia Regiment, 179

2nd Virginia Regiment, 174, 176, 179

4th Continental Light Dragoons, 180

8th Connecticut Regiment, 98

17th Regiment, 135

44th Regiment, 11, 57, 177

48th Regiment, 11

50th Regiment, 1, 5, 11, 17, 167

51st Regiment, 1, 11, 17, 167

60th Regiment, 144

80th Regiment, (see also Gage's Light Armed Foot), 29

Abercromby, James, 19, 23, 24, 49, 57, 122, 131

Alexander, William, 131

Allen, William, 136

Amherst, Jeffery, 23, 29, 31, 101, 121, 122, 128, 132, 145, 176

Anderson, William, 108

Anson, 170

Armstrong, John, 141, 143, 144

Babcock, Henry, 145

Bagley, Jonathan, 121

Barbar, James, 57, 58, 60

Barclay, David and Sons, 136

Barnard, Jonathan, 121

Barton, Thomas, 136

Beall, Benjamin, 109

Blair, John, 173, 174

Blodget, Samuel, 129

Board of Ordnance, 1, 20, 21, 29, 31, 33, 39, 41, 42, 65, 104, 118, 134, 149, 170

Boscawen, Edward, 170

Boscowen, 15, 26, 28

Bosomworth, Captain, 46

Boston Weekly News Letter, 155

Bouquet, Henry, 43, 104, 143, 144, 173, 174

Bowles, John, 151

Braddock, Edward, 11, 17, 19, 41, 109, 125, 131, 134, 136, 141, 167, 170, 177, 180

Bradstreet, John, 23

Bumford, John, 49, 50, 61, 62

Burd, John, 143

Bush, John, 45

Byrd, William III, 173, 174, 175, 176

Campbell, John the Earl of Loudon (see also Lord Loudon), 19, 104, 170

Charming Philley, 151

Clifford, Bejamin, 123

Clifford, William, 123

Cobbs, Samuel, 171

Cole, Benjamin, 27

Copley, John, 105

Creagh, Patrick, 108

Crown Point, 17, 25, 29, 118, 119, 121, 123, 127, 131

Dafte, John, 105, 106

Dagworthy, John, 109, 113, 114, 115

Dakin, Jonathan, 120

Delancy, James, 164

Delancy's (Oliver) Regiment, 132

Denny, William, 143

DePaiba, Rowland, 53

Dick, James, 113

Dinwiddie, Robert, Lt. Governor, 21, 125, 127, 131, 134, 164, 167, 170, 173, 179

Dobbs, Arthur, 133, 134, 135, 167

Dod, John, 155

Doty, Thomas, 120

Duychinck, Christopher, 132

Earl of Halifax, 127

Earl of Loudon, 135

East India Company, 136

Ellinger, Edmond, 153

Ellis, Henry, 103, 104

Faber, Johanes, 81, 84

Farmer and Galton, 164

Farmer, Ruth, 121

Farmer, William, 121

Fitch, Thomas, Governor, 100

Fitch, Thomas, Colonel, 119

Forbes, John, vii, 23, 24, 25, 43, 46, 113, 135, 141, 143, 144, 173, 174, 179

Forks of the Ohio, 135

Forts

    Beausejour, 117

    Cumberland, 174

    Dobbs, North Carolina, 135

    Duquesne, 11, 17, 23, 135, 136, 141

    Edward, 25, 101

    Frederick, Maryland, 111

    Frederick, Massachusetts (now Maine), 117

    Frontenac, 23

    George, New York, 131

    Granville, 141

    Ligonier, Pennsylvania, 144

    Loudon, Virginia, 135, 171, 173, 175, 176, 179

    Necessity, 11

    Niagra, 29, 127, 131

    Norris, 143

    Prince George, 155

    Ticonderoga, New York, 13, 14, 16, 23, 25, 26, 27, 29, 48, 119, 121, 132

    Vause, Virginia, 180

Fowle, Jacob, 119

Franklin, Benjamin, 136, 143

Furnis, James, 1, 19, 21, 25, 99, 101, 118, 119, 122, 123, 128, 132, 145

Gage's Light Armed Foot, 29

Goldsborough, Charles, 107

Grafton, 170

Grant, James, 158

Halkett, Peter, 177

Hancock, 49

Hardy, Charles, 131

Harris, John, 143

Hatcher, Thomas, 29, 30

Hawkins, John, 111

Hawley (II), Thomas of London, 137

Henry, Fort Loudon (Va) Armourer, 174, 175

Henshaw, William, 46

Hill, Jonathan, 143

Holler, Jacob, 125

Holt, Joshua, 122

Hulburt, Titus, 99

Innes, James, 111, 133

Johnson, Sir William, 31, 63

Johnston, John, 132

Jordan, Edward, 146

Julian, Isaac, 179

Keeny, Benjamin, 101

Kinman, William, 95

Kittanning, 144

Knox, John, 44

Lemon, John, 103

Lewis, Andrew, 165

Lewis, Josiah, 98

Lewis, Roger, 98, 99

Livinston, William, 132

Lord Calvert, 107

Lord Loudon, 19, 104, 170

Louisburg, 23

Loyal Judith, 103, 149

Luney, Peter, 180

Machault, 5

Mackall, J. J., 107

Marcy, Moses, 121

McClughan, John, 143

Melchoir, Leonard, 136

Mercer, George, 179

Miller, John, 143

Monarch, 170

Moore, Ruxton, 180

Morris, Robert Hunt, 137, 140, 141

Moses Marcy House, 121

North, Edward, 89, 90, 137, 138

Norton, John, 119

Noxon, Benjamin, 143

Ogle, Samuel, 108

Oglethorpe, James, 103, 104, 151

Parks, John, 97

Payson's Company (of Connecticut), 101

Peale, Charles Willson, 176

Pearson, Thomas, 134

Pepperell, Major General Sir WIlliam, 1

Peters, William, 141

Phips, Spencer, 100

Pitt, William, 23, 143, 144

Plolony, Lieutenant, 57

Pownall, Thomas, Governor, 119, 121, 122

Prior, Clothier, 101

Raines, Solomon, 119

Read, James, 136

Reynolds, John, Governor, 103, 104

Rhode Island Regiment, 145

Richards, Edward, 152

Robinson, Thomas, 167

Rogers, Benjamin, 165

Roosevelt, Nicolas, 132

Royal Artillery, 31

Schuyler, Peter, 131

Scott, George, 21, 118

Sharod/Georges, Thomas, 46

Sharp, Horatio, 109, 111, 113, 114, 133, , 174, 179

Shirley, William, 1, 17, 19, 20, 111, 117, 131, 137, 140, 170, 171

Simpson, Robert, 149

Smith, Charles, 135, 176

Smith, Samuel, 120

St. Clair, John, 105, 141, 173, 174, 177

Staples, William, 112

Starkey, Mr. of North Carolina, 134

Stephen, Adam, 176, 179

Stephens, Francis, 19, 35, 37

Stevenson, George, 141

Stewart, Robert, 175, 177, 179

Tayler, Mesach, 45

Thomson, Jacob, 47

Tingle, Samuel, 131

Torbay, 170

Tower of London, 1, 3, 19, 21, 25, 27, 31, 38, 103, 104, 109, 121, 133, 134, 136, 144, 173

Toye, John, 100

Travers, Major, 107

Turner, Ordnance Comptroller, 21, 170

Van Schaick, Gosen, 132

Vaughan, 24

Virginia Regiment, 165, 171, 173, 174, 176, 179

Waddle, Hugh, 135

Waggener, Thomas, 171

Wainset, Harper, 119

Washington, George, 11, 135, 171, 173, 174, 175, 176, 179, 180

Watkin, Rober, 69, 70, 178

Wells, Edmund, Captain, 101

Wells, S. Lieutenant, 101

West, William, 46, 144

White, Patrick, 108

Whiting, Nathan, 97

Whitney, Salmon, 121

Williams, Thomas, 119

Wilson, Richard, 41, 53, 69, 90, 103, 122, 124, 125, 126, 128, 132, 151, 153

Windham, William, iv, 89

Winslow, John, 21, 118, 123

Withers, William, 111

Wonslow's Company, 123

Young, Commissary, 143